# BREAKING THE BONDS OF RACISM

# BREAKING THE BONDS OF RACISM

by
Paul
and
Ouida
Lindsey

AN ETC PUBLICATION
1974

# CIP

Library of Congress Cataloging in Publication Data

Lindsey, Paul, 1924 -

Breaking the bonds of racism.

SUMMARY: Describes the lifestyle of blacks in the United States — including the problems of housing, economics, stereotypes — and the perspectives of both blacks and whites regarding education and learning.

Bibliography: p. 219

1. United States — Race question. 2. Negroes — Education. 3. School integration — United States. [1. United States — Race relations. 2. Negroes — Education. 3. School integration] I. Lindsey, Ouida, 1927 - joint author. II. Title.

E185.61.L573        301.45'19'6073        73-19820
ISBN 0-88280-007-8                            $8.95

Copyright © 1974 by  ETC PUBLICATIONS
18512 Pierce Terrace
Homewood, Illinois  60430

# CONTENTS

# ILLUSTRATIONS

*We dedicate this book*
*to all the people*
*who cared enough to ask . . . .*

# FOREWORD

Paul and Ouida Lindsey have written a remarkably useful and interesting book on the relations between blacks and whites in America. This gifted couple have kept the message clear and simple, but they are so competent with facts and feelings that even the very sophisticated student of race relations is bound to read their book with interest.

With seven years of experience leading discussions and teaching courses on race relations, and as writer of a newspaper column, Ouida Lindsey knows what children, young people, parents and teachers are puzzled about in black-white relationships. She is not hostile to whites, but neither does she spare them when recounting the damage they have done, especially to black children in this country.

The student of race relations will ask where the Lindseys stand on the issue of black separatism as against cultural pluralism — the two most active ideologies operating in this area. Clearly, they do not favor a separate group existence for blacks, a kind of American Bantustan. Also, they attribute many of the problems of black people to poverty and to the operation of discrimination against them rather than to something peculiar to "black culture." They favor racial integration in schools, in the economic and political life of the nation, and in residential areas.

But they opt for a kind of interactive pluralism, in which the various ethnic and racial groups maintain their own traditions, are proud of their group, but respect and understand the other cultures of this country. Therefore they do not have a simple melting-pot theory of the way they will go during the remainder of this century.

The book is certainly most useful to teachers, white and black, who want more information of a balanced kind. The last few chapters are aimed especially at educators, and contain much wisdom, with many concrete examples of failure and success among teachers and students as they try to work together across color lines. The first seven chapters give good background facts, interpretations, and answers to those who have questions about race, family, marriage, crime and ghetto life. Teachers will find lots of useful information on these topics. The chapter on Stereotypes is especially useful, dealing directly with some of the stereotypes about moral behavior that many liberal people try to ignore.

As I read this work, I thought how useful it would be if equally gifted and experienced persons of Spanish-American, Japanese-American, Chinese-American, Filipino and American Indian cultures would write parallel books.

Robert J. Havighurst
Professor of Education
    and Human Development
The University of Chicago

# AUTHORS' PREFACE

This book is an outgrowth of the interchange of questions and answers. The questions have been asked by several thousand people — elementary and high school students, graduate students in teaching, teachers and other adults in various walks of life. Answers have been supplied by Ouida in numerous assemblies, human relations seminars, discussion groups and school classes. In the beginning (in the early months of 1966) these various gatherings were of a spontaneous nature — interested teachers and/or students inviting Ouida to address their classes or meetings.

The format of the sessions was as follows: Questions to be discussed were obtained from the prospective audience prior to Ouida's appearance. The questions were then typed and mimeographed. Each member of the audience was given a list of questions and was free to ask either any question on the list or any questions other than those found on the list. This procedure was designed to put the audience at ease and elicit a maximum of audience participation. The questions could be stated or an individual could ask for a response to a question by indicating its listed number. Though an audience might be somewhat cool in the beginning, the sessions usually ended with an enthusiastic ovation and queries from many as to what they might do to help bring about more and better interracial associations and understandings.

The response to the sessions was gratifying. But, more importantly, these sessions revealed an apparent lack in the conventional education system of serious, dedicated concern with the problems of the various races and ethnic groups getting to know each other and living together in our complex society; of reaching the goal of an integrated and harmonious society devoid of racial hate.

At the time Ouida began engaging in the question-answer sessions, she was employed at the University of Chicago in the University's School of Education. As a result, she became acquainted with a number of graduate students in education. She was asked by several to give them some pointers, in writing, which could be of some help to those who would be teaching black students for the first time, and indeed, teaching for the first time, too. From their request resulted a booklet entitled *If You're Going to Teach Negro Students for the First Time . . .* by Ouida Lindsey and edited by Paul Lindsey. (At the time of writing the booklet the term "Black" had not yet replaced "Negro.") This booklet received much favorable comment from educators across the country. When Ouida mentioned this booklet in her column "For Real" which she writes weekly for the *Chicago Sun-Times,* hundreds of requests were received for copies. A slightly revised edition, *If You're Going to Teach Black Students for the First Time . . .* was prepared and more copies were mailed to meet the demand.

In 1968, the year of Martin Luther King, Jr.'s assassination and of further large-scale riots in the big-city ghettos, Ouida was invited by the then head of the Master of Arts in Teaching program, Mr. Kevin Ryan, at the University of Chicago, to conduct an elective course in race and cultural relations for the Graduate students. Ouida conducted this course until mid-1971 while at the same time giving much the same course to students in both the University elementary and high schools. During this period she also conducted the same type of course at Columbia College (whose curriculum is oriented toward communications media) in Chicago. She continues to offer this course at Columbia College as well as continuing to conduct race relations workshops for various groups: answering questions and making suggestions related to problems in race relations.

The thousands of questions asked — many of which recurred repeatedly in various audiences and which are still recurring among different groups — suggested to the authors that a book addressing itself directly to the questions would be of value. The first stage in the writing of the book was to go through the lists of questions and to categorize them under subject headings. Some of the questions have been taken from papers of students submitted to Ouida's courses on race relations.

Part I of the book deals with questions raised by people in all walks of life, and with which teachers and many other people are continually confronted. Part II deals more specifically with questions raised by teachers and prospective teachers concerned about teaching black students. Many of the questions asked specifically by the teacher groups are essentially the same as those asked by everybody else. Answers to teachers' questions (and those of administrators) are, however, dealt with as much as possible within the context of school situations.

We wish to express our indebtedness to the many people who have written about and worked in the cause of civil rights and harmonious race relations. It is our hope that this book will be considered one more step in the same direction they have taken before us.

Paul and Ouida Lindsey
Chicago, Illinois

# PART I

## THE LIFESTYLE

## OF BLACK PEOPLE

ONE

# OVERVIEW

*We have now announced that such segregation is a denial of the equal protection of the laws.* — Decision of the U.S. Supreme Court, May 17, 1954, *Brown vs. Board of Education.*

We are in a transitional period of human relations. A transition accompanied by much social confusion and turmoil; much psychological perplexity and anxiety.

Long standing legal barriers to participation and association of all Americans in political, economic, educational and cultural processes have been dismantled. The intentions of the 13th, 14th and 15th Amendments, through long and dedicated efforts of named and nameless people, have been embodied in Supreme Court decisions and congressional legislation.

The law of the land is clear — segregation is illegal; denial of due process and equal protection of the law are illegal. There is now no conflict between civil rights provisions of the constitution and judicial and legislative interpretation.

As to the social meaning of the legal imperatives, one could make statements about structural consequences to society, effects on patterns of behavior and role expectations, *mores* and their strain toward consistency or conflict, changing forms of social control, etc. But the meaning in simple terms is clear — the law permits and encourages human beings to treat each other with equality and respect; to associate and participate as equals with equal rights and opportunities.

Although legal barriers to equal rights and treatment have been removed, there remains reluctance among large numbers of citizens in many walks of life to accord their fellow citizens decency, respect, justice and dignity. State legislatures, such as that of Illinois, refuse to enact fair housing laws even in the face of a national fair housing

3

law; workers in skilled trades are opposed to accepting black workers in their ranks; parents oppose sending their children to school with children of different races, etc.

Presumably the founding unifying ideas of the country are and have been taught in the school systems. At least most school children are exposed at some time or another to the ringing phrases of the Declaration of Independence, Lincoln's Gettysburg Address, the Preamble of the Constitution, and the 13th, 14th and 15th Amendments. Yet for extremely large proportions of the population these ideas have not become practical values, vital components of peoples' behavior and attitudes toward others in the society. One can indeed wonder at the persistence and tenacity of more primitive, tribal notions as bases for judgements of other peoples' natures and deserts.

For instance, the primitive notion persists that because people are different, they are inferior or superior. This notion is of particular tenacity if the difference is one of skin color and hair texture. A little reflection would show that such a notion in itself is not deleterious. That is, one could conceivably hold that others are inferior but still be dedicated to the proposition that these others are entitled to equal opportunities for life, liberty, and the fullest possible development of their potentialities, that they should be accorded the normal amount of encouragement and help one would accord to those not considered inferior.

Such a course would run the risk that those to whom inferiority is ascribed would prove not to be inferior in abilities or attainments prized in our society. However, it is characteristic of man (1) that he likes to be secure in his notions, and (2) that he works toward producing visible, tangible proof of his cherished notions, so that they become valid to the beholder. (Social scientists refer to this as the self-fulfilling prophecy). Hence, the creation in the past of elaborate legal and social codes designed to deprive others of free and equal access to employment and education, to the utilization and consumption of a society's goods, services, and space.

Having by proscription and exclusion created a climate promoting inferior standards of living conditions and denial of opportunity to certain populations, we then stand aside and point to them proclaiming that the particular populations are, indeed, inferior. Why else don't they work like we do, take care of their kids, get an education, keep up their property and so on?

4

Having by proscription and exclusion created a climate promoting inferior standards of living and denial of opportunity to certain populations, we then stand aside and point to them proclaiming that the particular populations are, indeed, inferior. Why else don't they work like WE do, take care of their kids, get an education, keep up their property and so on?

Such are the consequences of dedication to the proposition that some men are created inferior to others. Try to imagine the misery and tragedy that would have been averted had our society dedicated itself with equal zeal to the proposition that all men are created equal.

Another characteristic of those who hold to the myth of inferiority is the reluctance to give up this notion despite facts indicating the contrary. When, despite the wholesale disabilities inflicted upon the proscribed group, men and women of the group attain levels of achievement valued in the society, this is not considered evidence of the group's essential equality; as evidence of achievement-potential which could be expanded under more favorable conditions.

The group as a whole is still held to be inferior, and successful individuals are regarded as curiosities. They are often subjected to an inverted form of flattery which regards them as "different" from their brethren. The intent of this code of behavior is to deny the person pride in his origins and to maintain the fiction of essential inequality. There are extremists who go to the length of accounting for significant achievements by blacks as due to their being part white, while at the same time decrying race mixture as "mongrelization" leading to a lower level of intelligence and culture.

However, black people (whatever their actual color or physiognomy) are refusing to passively accept socially imposed disabilities and derogatory status definitions. Slogans of "Black Pride" and "Black Power" have emerged representing assertions of dignity and the right to full participation in political and economic life. White people today are troubled about the meaning of such slogans.

White people are also troubled about riots in the cities' ghettos; about school boycotts and demonstrations by blacks demanding such things as Black Study Courses, removal of certain teachers, a voice in school administration, about black demands for

5

community control in ghetto areas, about black demands for remunerative employment and training for it, proportionate to their population.

They profess concern for "crime in the streets," by which is meant crime committed by blacks; for the large number of women in the ghetto who have out-of-wedlock children and receive public aid money; for the racial conflict between black and white students in the schools blacks and whites attend together. These are real and legitimate concerns, and they are shared by black and white alike.

Everyone is concerned about his own personal safety; about the safety of his children; and, about his children obtaining the best possible education unmolested. Teachers and parents alike are concerned about classroom size, discipline problems and everyone wants a classroom in which children can be taught in an atmosphere unhampered by these problems. Black parents in large cities are particularly concerned with this problem — to the extent that many who can afford to do so, educate their children either in costly private schools in the city or suburbs, or out of their state.

Following the ghetto riots of 1967 in many American cities, the *Report of the National Advisory Commission on Civil Disorders* was published. It is better known as the Kerner Report — after the then Governor of Illinois, Otto Kerner, Chairman of the Commission. The Report is exhaustive in describing ghetto conditions; it is clear in assigning causes for these conditions; and it is clear in its recommendations as to what must be done "compatible with the historic ideals of American society" to remedy these conditions.

The report notes that ghetto problems and the resulting disorders are not isolated problems of the black neighborhoods, but are symptomatic of endemic ills of our society — the fundamental ill being " . . . the racial attitude and behavior of white Americans toward black Americans . . . white racism is essentially responsible for the explosive mixture which has accumulated in our cities since the end of World War II. At the basis of this mixture are three of the most bitter fruits of white racial attitudes:

Pervasive discrimination and segregation . . .

Black migration and white exodus . . .

Black ghettos . . .

There it is — in black and white. We are reaping what has been sown.

OVERVIEW

In August 1966, at the Liberty Baptist Church in Chicago, filled to over-flowing with people, black, brown and white, just returned from marching in all-white neighborhoods, Dr. Martin Luther King, Jr., made a speech evaluating the events of the day and their meaning. He referred to the march participants as performing the role of social psychiatrists. The marchers had been vilified, taunted, pelted with rocks, eggs, cherry bombs, and presumably would have been assaulted *en masse* in the absence of disciplined police protection.

The marches were in behalf of open occupancy; their destinations were real-estate offices known to discriminate against non-whites in the sale and rental of housing, where short vigils were to be held. Hostility, of course, was known to exist, but the scale and vehemence of its expression was surprising. Those who had participated in the civil rights marches in southern states reported they had witnessed no fury in the southern marches exceeding or equaling that expressed by northerners. The hatred was out in the open where it at least could be confronted. There could be no mistaking the reason blacks were hemmed in ghettos after this display.

The meeting was memorable for yet another incident. Present in the audience and introduced by Dr. King were the parents of a teenage honor student who was beaten to death while standing on a corner waiting for a bus in the township of Cicero for no reason other than that he was black. He had gone to Cicero to look for employment. Cicero is an all-white town directly adjacent to Chicago and famous as the headquarters for Capone and his heirs. Of the bitter fruits of our attitudes, wanton killing of others is the bitterest.

This book is not about attitudes alone. Rather, it is about perceptions, conceptions and misconceptions which go to shape our beliefs and justify our attitudes. It might be considered a dialogue — or a confrontation.

Attitudes can be modified in individuals. And, of course, attitudes of generations change. Who today among men and women (perhaps a majority even of the latter were opposed to granting the vote to their own sex) questions the right, even the duty, of women to vote?

People today are curious and questioning about relations between the races — particularly young people. The stranger has

*"Buy yourselves guns and teach your wives to use them," an American Nazi Party Speaker tells a white crowd in Chicago.* (Chicago Daily News Photo)

come into the midst. Black people are more and more visible in positions and occupations where formerly they were hardly present — in banks, insurance companies, department stores, advertising, law, politics, the arts, sports, etc.

Not too many years ago, even in the Chicago community of Hyde Park, internationally famous as a liberal, innovative community, with more people per square foot with more academic degrees than any other community in the United States, few black people were to be seen in the white collar jobs and professions. Civil rights organizations were demanding that the bank bearing the name of the community, where black employees are now numerous and visible, hire and upgrade black people.

If in recent years black people have become increasingly visible in white collar jobs and professions, they have also become dramatically visible in the teeming city ghettos where they have been confined by discriminatory housing policies and hostile attitudes and behavior.

In the ghetto we see in concentration the many individual and social problems characteristic of the society in which we live. Unemployment, broken families, illegitimate births, families receiving public financial aid, crime, delinquency, illiteracy, mental illnesses, retardation, malnutrition, tuberculosis, veneral disease, etc. are certainly not peculiar to black ghettos of the cities. But undoubtedly, in ghettos the incidence of all these problems is higher.

Students of city patterns of life and growth have established and re-established connection between population density, poverty, lack of education, and high incidence of such problems among various ethnic groups. Novelists and poets have chronicled the bitterness, frustration, and despair of ghetto inhabitants and the consequent potential for violent outbursts. The Chicago riots of 1966 triggered by police shutting off water from a fire hydrant in which youngsters were splashing in hot summer weather, brought the ghetto of that city into full view. Inhabitants in the ghettos of Watts, Detroit, and elsewhere throughout the nation have demonstrated their unhappiness with their living conditions. Hostility toward whites has surfaced because whites are largely perceived by the ghetto dwellers as responsible for their plight.

Viewing the problems of our cities brought explosively to the surface, the Kerner Report has expressed concern about development of "polarization" — by which is meant, essentially, perpetuation of hostile attitudes with the consequence of expanding ghettos and ghetto problems. In regard to the problem of "polarization," the zoologist Desmond Morris has drawn the following important conclusion:

> Once the harm has been done . . . the only possible hope of preventing a further spread of . . . hostility must be founded on personal inter-change and knowledge of . . . the other individuals *as individuals*. (orig. itals.) If this does not happen, then the inter-group hostility will harden and the green-haired individuals — even those who are non-violent — will feel the need to club together and defend one another. Once this has occurred, the real violence is just around the corner."

Personal interchange and knowledge of others as individuals obviously presume association, although mere association does not guarantee that interchange, knowledge, and understanding will result. Emergence of increased areas of association, particularly in employment and education, provide opportunity for interchange and getting to know one another. However, even in these areas meaningful interchange is too often stifled by preconceptions of others and inhibitions in bringing out into the open the assumptions upon which the preconceptions are based. But people do want to know and they are full of honest and rather frank questions. It is certainly a function of our educational system to provide honest and frank answers.

Education, by definition, is a good, and it is, of course, not confined to the formality of a school system.

But the school system can do much good or ill. All childrens' and young peoples' lives are touched in our society by it. To know that in ghetto schools, e.g., in the city of Chicago, the average reading level of eighth grade pupils is nearly three years below the national average eighth grade reading level, is appalling. To know that most of the pupils in schools are not being taught about each other, about the need to, and the how to live with each other is equally appalling. These two conditions are certainly not unrelated.

It is hoped this book will be of value to those interested in or confronted with problems of transition from a segregated to an integrated society. Perhaps some inspiration will be found in it for

## READING LEVEL COMPARISON OF CHICAGO SCHOOL CHILDREN
## IN GHETTO AND NON GHETTO SCHOOLS
## WITH NATIONAL AVERAGES

The graph shows how the performance of Chicago public school pupils on standardized reading tests grows relatively poorer as the pupils move up through the grades.   The solid line shows the national average   —   each child gains another month in reading ability for each month in school.   The line below it shows the performance of an average pupil in an average Chicago public school.   The bottom line shows the performance of an average pupil in a typical inner-city school.

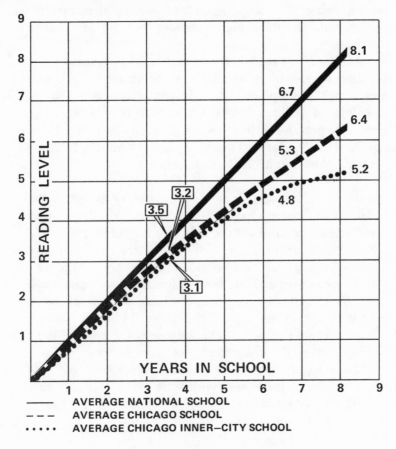

**FIGURE 1–1**

FROM: CHICAGO SUN-TIMES, JUNE 17, 1971

11

initiating programs of interracial communication which are not rendered sterile by abstract preconceptions and accompanying inhibitions.

Gunnar Myrdal has remarked of the educated middle-class American, that he knows of the miserable conditions under which millions of his compatriots live but "only in an abstract sort of way, not as a living reality." And to Myrdal it remains "something of a mystery that the majority of Americans show such a lack of concern about it all" particularly in view of their reputation for "Christian neighborliness." Probably the answer to the "mystery" is that segregation has done its work too well, corrupting a level of our emotional being not susceptible to fundamental alteration by mere sophistication. The following pages aim to avoid pretensions and sophistication.

Should any of our readers be staunch segregationists opposed to integration trends, we hope they may be struck by a spark that ignites a new "hot place" in their consciousness — to use the phraseology of William James. Conversion is possible.

The value premise of this work is probably best stated in words taken from the "I Have a Dream" speech of Martin Luther King, Jr., during the March on Washington:

> I still have a dream. It is a dream deeply rooted in the American Dream. I have a dream that one day this nation will rise up and live out the true meaning of its creed: We hold these truths to be self-evident that all men are created equal . . . I have a dream that one day . . . the sons of former slaves and the sons of former slave owners will be able to sit down together at the table of brotherhood . .
> I have a dream that my . . . children will one day live in a nation where they will not be judged by the color of their skins but by the content of their characters.
> I have a dream that one day . . . little black boys and girls will be able to join hands with little white boys and girls as sisters and brothers . . . Let freedom ring. And if America is to be a great nation this must be true.

*March on Washington, D.C. — Leaders of the March on Washington lock arms and put hands together as they move along Constitution Avenue August 28, 1963. R. Philip Randolph, march director, is at right, and Roy Wilkins, executive secretary of the National Association for the Advancement of Colored People (NAACP), is second from right. The Rev. Martin Luther King is seventh from right.   (UPI Photo)*

# TWO

# THE GHETTO: WHAT IT'S LIKE

*It's an everyday thing in the ghetto . . . only the strong survive.* From a popular song heard on juke boxes in the ghetto.

The term ghetto originated in Europe several hundred years ago to describe an area in which Jews lived. One theory is that the term is derived from the Italian *gietto*, a cannon foundry in Venice near which the first Jewish settlement was located in the Middle Ages. In European history, the ghetto became a place of involuntary confinement for Jews, maintained by strict laws of segregation, in every European country.

Some years ago, an area of an American city where black people lived was referred to as the "black belt"; but in recent years the term "ghetto" has taken its place. As far as black neighborhoods are concerned, the historic meaning of the word "ghetto" is particularly accurate in describing black areas of living. "Involuntary confinement" is just as true today, for most blacks, as it was for most Jews years ago.

The existence of a ghetto enables people to reinforce their stereotypes and caricatures of others. It serves as a concrete representation of fears and prejudices. People can point to the ghetto and say: "See, that's how they live, they like it that way!" while intensive, massive efforts are made to prevent those who wish to leave the ghetto behind from doing so.

What is the ghetto? What are the people like who live there? Why don't people who live there keep up their property? Why is there so much crime, so many prostitutes, addicts, illegitimate births? These kinds of questions are asked continually by students. They are also asked by people with academic degrees who have been exposed to courses in the social sciences. Even many people who staff our welfare and educational systems profess they cannot see why people in the ghetto live the way they do; while at the same time assuming the attitude that not much can be done with those from such a deprived background. This attitude can be harmful, leading, as it often does, to negative and punitive behavior toward ghetto children and their parents.

The mistake should not be made of assuming that because a black lives in the ghetto he is backward, ignorant, or deprived.

The ghetto is not all slum. There are nice well-kept homes occupied by people with middle-class standards which sometimes are side-by-side with buildings which are fast deteriorating. To further complicate the picture, whole blocks of well-kept owner occupied housing can be found adjacent to or surrounded by slum apartment buildings or kitchenettes. These residents are victimized by encroaching deterioration of neighborhood property and services as well as by the growth of delinquent and criminal depredations. Also, it should be pointed out that not all the poorer people (including those on public aid) of the ghetto occupying slum dwellings are dissolute and without middle-class standards of decency and aspiration.

There are also the areas of almost solid black middle-class family occupancy, with blocks on blocks of neat, modest homes fronted by green lawns and trees. Because of proximity to the inner ghetto and school districting policies, children of these families suffer the effects of overcrowded school conditions and harassment by gangs.

Questions asked as to why "they" live the way they do, etc., arise from stereotyping "all" black people with the kinds of behavior so dramatically evident in the large poverty areas of the cities. The inner city ghettos do indeed harbor much disorganized, pathological, and anti-social behavior. The Reverend James G. Jones, Jr., founder of St. Leonard's House, a rehabilitation home for released prisoners in Chicago, worked many years in the ghetto. He has remarked in an article entitled "I Found I Hadn't Left the Prison At All," appearing in the magazine *Poverty and Health*, March, 1969:

> I can top every story you can tell me about the ghetto because what you say is true. The ghetto is no great place to live. But the question is, why is this so.

*In the ghetto, the tragedy of the young is the greatest. Members of the Barons, a teen-age gang, huddling across from Taylor Homes in Chicago.* (Chicago Daily News Photo)

17

# THE LIFESTYLE OF BLACK PEOPLE

## Crime in the Street

Crime, and particularly crime in the streets, has in recent years loomed large in the ghetto and fringe areas. Few days go by that we don't read in the newspapers of gangs and gang warfare in the ghetto; of young men killing each other; of robberies, beatings and killings of ordinary citizens. One sees in the ghetto gang names painted throughout the area on walls of thousands of buildings — such names as *Maniacs, Apache, Black Prince, Satans, Disciples, Cobras, Lords, Vice Lords, Blackstone Rangers, Black P. Stone Nation* and statements such as "Stone Run It" or "Maniac Run It." Following is a description of the gang phenomenon:

> Every corner has its gang, not always on the best terms with the rivals in the next block, but all with a common program: defiance of law and order, and with a common ambition: to get 'pinched', i.e. arrested, so as to pose as heroes before their fellows. A successful raid on the grocer's till is a good mark, 'doing up' a policeman cause for a promotion. The gang is an institution . . . The gang is the ripe fruit of tenement house growth. It was born there, endowed with a heritage of instinctive hostility to restraint . . . [The] tough represents the essence of reaction against the old and the new oppression, nursed in the rank soil of [the] slums . . . They reflect exactly the conditions of the tenements from which they sprang. Murder is as congenial to . . . Street as quiet to . . . Hill . . . The guillotine Paris set up . . . to avenge its wrongs was not more relentless, or less discriminating than [the gangs]. The difference is of intent. Murder with that was the serious purpose; with ours it is the careless incident, the wanton brutality of the moment. Bravado and robbery are the real purposes of the gangs; the former prompts the attack upon the policeman, the latter upon the citizen. Within a single week last spring, the newspapers reported six murderous assaults on unoffending people committed by young highwaymen on the public streets . . .

The writer goes on to say of the young offender that if his actions

> helped to make manifest that all effort to reclaim his kind must begin with the conditions of life against which his very existence is a protest, even the tough has not lived in vain. This measure should be accorded him, that with or without his good-will he has been a factor in urging battle against the slums that bred him.

The above account was written in 1890 by Jacob Riis in his book *How the Other Half Lives.* It is concerned with conditions in New York. The gangs he spoke of were composed predominantly of second generation Irish, German, and English. But the account today would be the same for the slum areas, simply substituting black young men who are largely second generation to the large cities. It should be apparent that crime in the streets is neither new nor peculiar to a racial group but is generated by the same kinds of conditions. Black youth engage in the same kind of anti-social behavior for much the same reasons as whites.

The majority of people in the ghetto are not given to criminal depredations. But the inhabitants of the ghettos account for most of the victims of violent crimes committed. The ghetto is not a great place to live. According to the report of the *National Commission on the Causes and Prevention of Violence,*

> There is a widespread public misconception that most violent crime is committed by black offenders against white victims. This is not true . . . The majority of these crimes involve blacks attacking blacks, while most of the remainder involves whites victimizing whites. Indeed, our Survey found that 90% of urban homicides, aggravated assaults, and rapes involve victims and offenders of the same race.

(The report notes that robbery has a fairly high interracial score with 45% of robberies being committed by blacks against white men). The report also quotes an expert who stated that in Chicago a person living in the inner city faced a risk each year of 1 in 77 of being assaulted. In the better areas of the city the risk was 1 in

2,000, and in the rich suburbs 1 in 10,000. People living in high risk areas of the city desire the freedom to move out of the ghetto; desire to live where their children will not be exposed to and victimized by large numbers of delinquents, just as non-ghetto dwellers feel. But racism, with its resultant patterns of forced containment, has prevented people who wish to do so from moving out of slum environs, and escaping the fear created by gang beatings and killings.

At the turn of the century, the German and the Irish accounted for the greatest amount of delinquency and gang activity; later in the century, Polish and Italian youth achieved this dubious distinction. As members of these ethnic groups moved out of the slum areas they occupied and dispersed throughout the city and suburbs, the delinquency rate for those of the group remaining in the old areas also dropped. So long as our attitudes of hostility persist in preventing free movement from the ghetto, resulting in continued confinement in areas on the basis of color or presumed race, so long will the conditions exist for flourishing crime and delinquency.

## Housing

"The ghetto is no great place to live," to again repeat Reverend Jones' phrase. Living arrangements in the ghetto are characterized by high density population; with over-crowding in dilapidated, deteriorating structures. A study made in Chicago by the Cook County Department of Public Aid revealed that less than half of public assistance families lived in sound housing. It was found that six-tenths of the families occupied quarters with building code violation. Many families were forced to share the bath facilities while two-thirds of the buildings were receiving either fair or poor maintenance services. Housing in general was described as bleak and deficient. Though the study was confined to families receiving public aid, many families not on aid reside in the same buildings. What is true of Chicago is typical of large metropolitan centers elsewhere throughout the nation.

Characteristic of the ghetto has been the kitchenette apartments housing large numbers of families. In more recent years problems associated with concentrations of lower income people in inadequate living space have been compounded by highrise public housing projects. There is one housing project in Chicago which contains 30,000 people in an area of less than two square miles; and it is in a row with other large projects.

A kitchenette building is one whose apartments have been cut up into smaller apartments, often with community baths and/or kitchens. Some of these buildings are well kept (i.e., clean, neat, well-painted, with regular garbage pick-up service, etc.). The majority, however, are shabby, run-down affairs, whose owners do not live in the buildings, or even in the neighborhood. The buildings generally have little or no janitorial services, irregular garbage pick-up service, plaster falling from the ceilings, huge cracks in the walls, bad flooring that splinters easily, bad or no hall lighting, bad plumbing — sometimes only cold water. There are too many families and too many children for the allotted space in a particular building, no trees or grass, broken windows and screens, rodents and roaches.

There is oftentimes lack of sufficient food among the families, and, among some, indifference to bodily cleanliness. The children in these buildings may see drunkeness, cruelty, indifference on one or both parents' faces, or that of their close neighbors. Many families who live in these buildings are decent and have so-called middle-class values and are *not* deprived; others in the same building *are* deprived; some families are receiving "aid", and some are not; and some families consist of both parents and children, while others have only one parent with the children.

Sometimes there are as many as five families, with as many children per each, sharing the same bathroom. Try to imagine that, on a school morning, with some adults getting ready to go to work, while the children are trying to get washed and dressed for school. Or imagine several families sharing a community kitchen — the one room on a floor that wasn't converted into an apartment and where everyone has to cook and eat.

In a kitchenette building each family must share a common door-bell, by being allotted a certain number of posted rings. For instance, a floor on one side of the building could have seven kitchenettes. The first apartment would have one ring and the following apartments graduating rings ending with the seventh

*Hotel sign advertising a Kitchenette.* (Chicago Daily News Photo)

*Padlocks are often placed on Kitchenette mailboxes in ghetto buildings to guard against pilfering. Loose wires are shown above the mail boxes.* (Sun-Times Photo)

having seven rings. Everyone must stop whatever he or she is doing at the time in order to count the number of rings which determine "for whom the bell tolls." Pandemonium can be created when someone rings more rings than apartments; or pauses too long between rings.

These buildings are usually equipped with what are called "crash panels" located at one end of the hallway of each floor, and/or fire escapes on the side of the building. The "crash panels" of yesteryear were sometimes opaque panes of glass framed in a wooden door which displayed large red printed words "Knock This Glass Out In Case of Fire." Usually the "crash panel" led into an apartment whose windows opened onto a porch or fire-escape.

For black people with low incomes, decent housing at reasonable rentals is very difficult to obtain. There is, nationwide, a shortage of adequate housing for the needs of the population; and in the big city ghettos the situation is acute. The agency of government concerned with the provision of adequate housing for the population (Department of Housing and Urban Development) has, during the last couple of decades, torn down more of the dwellings of the poor that it has built for them; thus increasing the pressures and tensions of ghetto living.

Many people wonder about the high-rise public housing projects which have been built and the black people who live there. Why do blacks who live there dislike them so, and why (since these buildings are obviously newer and better than the run-down buildings the tenants moved from) do they not take better care of them?

The answer to the first part of the question is simply that the black families living there are constantly afraid of strangers and gangs and look forward to the time they can move out. In the old torn down buildings in which they used to live, the danger was less, because the buildings were smaller and everyone knew everyone else and the stranger was highly visible. While in the hi-rise project buildings, which can reach 25 floors, families keep pretty much to themselves. Doors are kept locked and if screams are heard, most tenants do not bother calling the police because they believe their call will go unheeded or that the police will arrive much too late to save someone. Here the stranger is practically invisible, not only because of the constant flow of large numbers of persons, but because it is dangerous to make inquiries as to who a person is and what business he is on.

24

*Three children in a family of 10 are shown huddling in the kitchen to obtain warmth, the only room in the apartment with heat. Ice is on the floor from broken pipes in the bathroom.* (Chicago Daily News Photo)

# THE LIFESTYLE OF BLACK PEOPLE

There was an elderly lone matron kept captive in her own apartment in a Chicago hi-rise for days by three members of a gang, whose daily assaults on her finally prompted a neighbor to investigate which lead to her rescue and their capture by the police.

Many mothers will only allow their children to play on the walk-way, just outside of their respective doors. This is because if anything should happen to their children down in the playlots (even with the mother watching from the window), there is no way to prevent or stop the action. By the time the mother could reach the ground level, whatever was happening would be over.

A complaint that mothers sometimes voice is that there usually are no toilet facilities on the ground level for their children at play in the playlots to use. As a result, some of the children find it easier to simply use the elevators instead of having an accident on the way to their families' apartment located on some upper floor. In some of the projects, families with both parents in the home and not receiving welfare live either on one side or on certain floors of a building. Segregated from these families are those whose father or mother is absent from the home and who may or may not receive aid from the welfare department.

This often leads to jealousies and snubs between such families living in the project. Also children of families not living in a project will sometimes look down on the children who do, ignoring them, not inviting them to get-togethers, etc. Such occurrences contribute to still more unrest within the project buildings.

There really is no choice as to the kind of neighbors one would wish to live near. There is no opportunity to live in surroundings that offer many different kinds of people, races, cultures, backgrounds. There are no concentrated areas dedicated to individual cultural growth; usually no art shops, libraries, beaches, theatres, or attractive safe places for teens to gather for productive purposes. Since the children and young adults have nothing exciting to see or do, they may congregate around the entrances to the buildings, on the corners, in front of stores to talk, to horse around, to have fun. Other children and adults are fearful of passing these large groups to go either into these tall buildings or out of them. "The majority of children standing around will do them no harm, but there are always the ones who will "show off" or need money and have no scruples about how they acquire it; or who

*Lone boy walks into a project.* (Chicago Daily News Photo)

have so much hate inside that they will attack anything that moves, and that's where the trouble starts.

"Why don't parents make their children come in at a certain time, so that those who have to be out will be safe coming into the buildings?" The answer is that many of the people in these projects do just that. However, there are some parents who were so used to allowing their children to "stay out in front of the house" when they lived in smaller buildings, that the habit persists even though they are now in a hi-rise project. When vast numbers of people, experiencing the same kinds of poverty-filled backgrounds, socially and economically, are crammed together like so much cordwood, there is no real chance to *live* differently than before.

In situations like this, if there are four thousand adults living in a three square block area, then there are at least fifteen thousand children living there too. They are going to mark-up buildings, fences, and so on. They are going to swing on trees, break glass, pull fixtures off the walls (either to sell or fight with), play on the grass, urinate (or worse) in the elevators, and beat each other up. And they can be of *any* color, race, creed, or nationality. No matter how it seems or looks, the *majority* of children living in this kind of building are not deliberately doing damage. But because there are so many that do, it is easy to overlook the fact that the vandals are a distinct minority.

Here are some comments of a working mother living with her husband and children in a high-rise project:

> My husband and I both work so our children can go to school far away from where we live. We keep them away from home as much as possible because of the awful things that go on around here. This winter kids have packed broken glass into snowballs and slammed them into other kids' faces.
>
> Three days ago, as I was leaving the building to go to work, I was hit with rotten eggs. They splattered my skin and clothes, but I was very grateful as I went back to our apartment to change . . . I could have been hit with a bottle instead. Can you imagine the impact of a bottle or a plastic bag of water hitting you from a falling distance of 15 floors?

*A man carries an open switchblade knife for protection as he starts to board a high rise elevator in a project.* (Chicago Daily News Photo)

When we all get home there is no rest for us. I have to pick my way through the kids in the area-ways. Once inside, the noise is so loud it's impossible to concentrate, let alone get uninterrupted sleep.

Because there's no supervision of the children [in the play areas outside the buildings] you're scared to send them downstairs to play. So they have to play in the area just outside their parents' apartments. But mixed in with them are teenagers and young men who drink wine, gamble, smoke marijuana, curse, fight and beg. They mug each other and the younger kids as well as the passing adults. Our apartment has been broken into four times and we've found who did it. If you hear someone yelling for help and you call the police, they won't come up in here. The police seldom come inside and how can you really blame them? It's horrible in here.

Did you ever have to walk up more than 10 flights of stairs mostly in the dark while carrying two shopping bags of groceries? Well, I did last night, and by the time I got in my apartment I was so scared my teeth were chattering. The elevators were broken. They are always being stalled or not working, but even when they work you're afraid to use them. Sometimes a stranger stops the elevators between floors to mug and rob you.

We moved here because we thought it would be better than what we had. But in the old building we at least knew who lived there and who didn't. Not so in the projects. So you mind your own business and try to get out as soon as you can.

James L. is a 12 year old boy who has "escaped" from one of the vertical cages called projects. James has been beaten several times by members of one of the gangs that roam the neighborhood surrounding the high-rise building where he lives. The point of the beatings was to coerce him into joining the gang. During the time of the last beating he was told that he would be killed if he did not soon become one of them. His parents finally decided to send him to an aunt who lives in a better and somewhat integrated neighborhood who consented to make room for him. James said:

I'm glad to be out of there. Man, you can stand out in front of my aunt's house late at night and stretch your arms wide open and nobody shoots at you . . . They shoot at everything there [in the project]. You, too, if you get in the way.

. . . most of the gangs don't believe in school and they think anybody who goes is stupid and ought to get ripped off . . . they say that after you graduate you can't even get a job . . . But I want to go, because I'm going to be a doctor.

James misses his parents and occasionally sneaks over to see them. Small for his age, thin, with a bitter-chocolate complexion, he is a very serious young man.

The city of St. Louis, recognizing that the huge Pruitt-Igoe housing project was a very bad human and social investment, demolished a large portion of it with dynamite. Perhaps so drastic a solution is not everywhere indicated. For instance, high rise public housing projects located (as many of them are) near educational and medical institutions could be used for housing professional people and their families as well as for students and various businesses. This would involve moving most of the present population out of the projects to housing scattered throughout the metropolitan area; a process which would help in raising the cultural and economic level of the cities. It is something to think about.

Living conditions of the nature described are breeding grounds for antisocial and immoral behavior. This is nothing new in the process of urban development; only our displacement value is new. The black man is now the troublesome scapegoat. In the early years of this century the emigration of Slavic and Southern Europeans to this country was deplored by those who considered themselves natives. The newcomers were considered to be inferior to other Americans such as those of German, English, or Irish stock. They were accused of lowering the moral tenor of the country. They were characterized as those who filled the jails and asylums of the nation. This was "proof" of their inferiority. Assimilated descendants of these alleged inferior people now express the same kinds of negative attitudes toward black people.

*Man and woman walking up 15 flights of stairs in a hi-rise due to elevator not being repaired for nearly a month.* (Chicago Daily News Photo)

In the mid- and late nineteenth century both the German and the Irish groups were deplored as troublesome, undersirable elements. A committee of the New York Assembly investigating conditions in New York City tenement districts reported that landlords preferred to rent to blacks rather than to Irish or German poor in the better class of buildings, because, as Richard O'Connor points out in his book *The German-Americans: An Informal History:*

> . . . the incentive of possessing comparatively decent quarters appearing to inspire the colored residents with more desire for personal cleanliness and regard for property than is impressed upon the whites of their condition . . .

Newspapers of the time decried the danger in the streets because of the hooliganism of the German and the Irish.

Later in the century Jacob Riis reported (quoting from the *Real Estate Record*) that agents preferred Negro tenants to the lower class of foreign born because of their orderliness, cleanliness, and care for property.

So much for the association of desirable or undersirable behavior traits in regard to respect of property and persons with a particular ethnic or racial group. One thing however has remained constant — exploitation of blacks by landlords and real estate agents. The turn-of-the-century real estate men explained that in addition to Negroes being more desirable tenants, they could be charged higher rents. In the modern ghetto vernacular, this kind of behavior is referred to as the "rip off."

### Consumers

The rip off, or what in the area of consumerism might be called the "captive buyer lock-in," remains a characteristic of ghetto living. Here are two examples of the kinds of situations black people of low incomes experience in their daily lives:

> Mrs. Williams shops at a small grocery store in her neighborhood. One day she didn't have enough money to

pay for all she needed to purchase. The grocer told her not to worry, he'd be willing to give her credit any time she needed it. He pulled out a large ledger book and a small black book which he gave to Mrs. Williams, telling her to keep a record of her purchases in her book; and he would keep a record in his ledger. One day she came to pay her bill and the grocer added $20.00 to the amount Mrs. Williams had recorded in her little book. She maintained the grocer was mistaken, but he pulled out his ledger and said his amount was correct, that perhaps one of her children made purchases without telling her; though she knew the grocer would not have sold to her children without a note from her.

Mrs. Williams felt she had no recourse but to pay the grocer on his terms. She works as a matron in a hospital and has several children for whom she's the sole support. She knew that she would continue to need credit from time to time; and it seemed easier to continue to shop where she knew she could always get food when she ran short. This anecdote was related to several now middle-class black people who remembered well from their childhood the double bookkeeping game practiced by groceries and liquor stores. They were surprised to learn that the practice is still continuing.

The second example had a much more dramatic outcome, resulting in a consumer boycott action by Southside Chicago residents:

One afternoon on three different occasions, three children from the same family bought a bottle of pop at the same store. Each child was charged a different price for the same drink. When the children's mother learned of this she went to the store owner to complain. He was rude and told her she could take her business elsewhere. Angered, the woman reported the incident to her block club. As a result, the club decided to bring the matter to the attention of PUSH (People United to Save Humanity), a civil rights group.

The store was located in a block-long, convenient shopping area called Farmers Market. Stores were open to the sidewalk with various produce displayed in front of the stores and on the sidewalk. The area had the air of a wholesale market, and this was an attraction to customers. People became aware, however, that prices were quite high for the quality offered. Moreover, sanitary conditions were deplorable. When the situation was brought out into the open by PUSH, many people reported instances of insulting behavior toward them by the merchants, and filthy conditions they observed in the stores. PUSH organized demonstrations and an effective consumer boycott, centering largely on unsanitary conditions which were clearly in violation of City Board of Health regulations. The merchants were most reluctant to sanitize and modernize their facilities, complaining lack of funds. Many finally closed due to the effectiveness of the boycott action.

This latter example is an illustration of how one small incident can bring to light and set off dramatic protest against a situation of abuse long-suffered by people in the ghetto.

### Ghetto Families

The general impression of those who have never lived in the ghetto seems to be that most of the children are illegitimate, and that black families accept illegitimacy very easily. This is far from an accurate view. Even though the illegitimate child ratio is higher among blacks than among whites, black people in the kind of society which we share, feel unhappy about it as do others in our American culture. Illegitimate pregnancies and births are frowned upon by many blacks in the ghetto. It does not matter whether they are poor or well-to-do, either. As among whites, there are varying degrees of acceptance and censure of the unwed mother, and as of late, the unwed father.

Illegitimate births as well as crime, hopelessness, riots, etc., are largely by-products of poverty and segregation. Since blacks have more poverty than whites, they have proportionately more illegitimacy. Actually, the ghetto is characterized by a number of types of families. It is particularly important that school teachers and administrators realize that students in ghetto schools are likely to reflect the entire range of family types existing in the general society.

Following are some examples of kinds of family situations from which students may come:

(a) *Mother and father in the home legally married.* All children born of these parents.

(b) *Mother and father in the home.* Common-law relationship. All children born of this mother and father.

(c) *Mother in the home.* All her children born out-of-wedlock; children may have different fathers.

(d) *Mother in the home.* Mother has children by legal husband who has left home, divorced, legally separated. Has other children born out-of-wedlock.

(e) *Mother in the home.* All children by same father. Father deserted, mother never legally married the father.

(f) *Mother in the home.* Widowed. All children by same father.

(g) *Grandmother and/or grandfather in the home.* Grandchildren legitimate. Orphaned due to death, illness, imprisonment, abandonment.

(h) *Grandmother and/or grandfather in the home.* All the grandchildren born out-of-wedlock. Orphaned due to death, illness, imprisonment, or abandonment.

(i) *Father in the home.* Mother deceased or deserted. All children by legally married mother and father.

There are other combinations involving aunts, uncles, cousins, friends, and legal guardians, but they would simply parallel the above examples. Also, any other groups of people in our world can and do reflect these combinations of family life. The family situation, Case (c) above, is the kind regarding blacks about which most people seem to have heard; and which many apparently believe is typical. This, however, is not the case.

According to census figures, 69% of all black families are headed by males and 31% by females. But the figures also reveal a dramatic correlation between poverty and female headed households. In the income level under $3,000 per year, 40% of households are headed by males and 60% by females; over $3,000 and up to $5,000, 54%

# THE GHETTO: WHAT IT'S LIKE

## PERCENTAGE OF BLACK HOUSEHOLDS HEADED BY MALES
## IN RELATION TO INCOME LEVEL

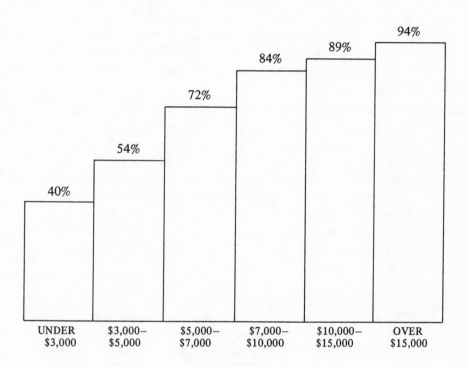

**INCOME**

**FIGURE 2–1**

Source: SOCIAL AND ECONOMIC STATUS OF THE BLACK POPULATION
IN THE U.S., SERIES P–23, BUREAU OF THE CENSUS, 1971

are headed by males, 46% by females; from $5,000 up to $7,000, the figures are respectively, 72% and 28%; $7,000 to $10,000, 84% and 16%; $10,000 to $15,000, 89% and 11%; over $15,000, 94% and 6%.

The figures speak for themselves, but are further illuminated by the following observation made by the late Oscar Lewis in his book, *La Vida:*

> To men who have no steady job or other source of income, who do not own property and have no wealth to pass on to their children, who are present-time oriented and who want to avoid the expense and legal difficulties involved in formal marriage and divorce, free union or consensual marriage makes a lot of sense.

> Women will often turn down offers of marriage because they feel it ties them down to men who are immature, punishing and generally unreliable. Women feel that con-sensual union gives them a better break; it gives them some of the freedom and flexibility that men have. By not giving the fathers of their children legal status as husbands, the women have a stronger claim on their children if they decide to leave their men. It also gives women exclusive rights to a house or any other property they may own.

It should not be assumed even in high poverty areas that all or most of the children are from fatherless households. Thomas Hopkins, a social worker, writing in the January 1973 issue of *Social Work*, remarks that teachers generally assume that a black child's mother is the only one to talk to about the child. Many teachers assume that the mother is single and the head of the family. Notes children bring home from school are usually addressed "Miss", he says.

But let us look at a hypothetical situation of Case (c) to see how it came about; and just why a young woman would find herself with a number of illegitimate children. The hypothetical case name will be Jean. Here is her story:

> Jean became pregnant at the age of 16 and dropped out of school. At this time, 1949, Jean's mother, Mrs. Jones, is

only 31 years old and has three young children of her own, ages 10, 12 and 14. She can't let her daughter and new grandchild live with her because there is not enough room or money. Also, Mrs. Jones' neighbors gossip about her daughter's "condition" and are snubbing her, as well as Jean. As a result, there is a lot of unhappiness in the family.

Jean has to go on Public Aid because there is no one to take care of her baby, and she has no skills. She gets a kitchenette apartment and tries to imitate her mother.

She is only sixteen years old, and she suddenly finds herself thrust into an adult world. She cannot have the friends she had before she became pregnant. Their parents will not let them keep up the friendship because Jean is a "bad girl." Mrs. Jones has her own problems, and no energy to devote much time to the problems of her daughter. The man in question cannot marry Jean perhaps because he is too young, has to help out at home, or is married already, or thinks the baby isn't his, or they don't love each other, or she just doesn't want to marry him, or a thousand reasons. Whatever the reason, she and her baby are alone.

She is still a child with a woman's problems. She wants to have fun and go out and do the things she believes adults do. By the time she is 33 in 1967, she has seven children. Their ages are 18, 17, 15, 13, 11, 8 and 7.

Let's examine Jean's background. How did this happen to her? How about her parents?

Mrs. Jones, Jean's mother, was born somewhere in the rural south. Her parents who had little or no schooling, were very poor, God-fearing people, who lived more or less on a day to day existence. Mrs. Jones, along with her siblings, was pulled out of school as soon as she could help in the fields. It just didn't matter if the chidren returned to school.

Mrs. Jones married and started her family at the age of 16 in 1934. She and her husband moved north because opportunities seemed better there. Her husband was the age as she. By 1942, she was 24 years old and had four children, ages 2, 7, 5, and 8; her husband dies while the last child was on the way.

Between 1934 and 1941, wives stayed home with the children. Jobs were scarce but they were more scarce for women. That meant mother was home more. The children were closely supervised. If mother went to the store, the neighbor reported to her what the children had done while she was gone, and if the report was a bad one, they were punished. Police officers were held in high respect by the adults, so the children respected them also. Teachers were considered as above reproach and woe to the child who brought home a note that mentioned some lack of respect, no homework done, "acting-up" in class, and so on. If he had been punished in school, he was punished again at home. All adults were treated with respect — or else! Black mothers and fathers had learned from their parents that certain individuals must be respected and this they taught their children.

In 1942 the war was on and labor was scarce, so that meant more black people could get better jobs with better pay than ever before. Women, black as well as white, could get jobs paying the same and sometimes more than the men. So that pulled the black mother from her home and put the children on their own. It was impossible to find someone to take care of the youngsters while the mother worked (there was more money to be made elsewhere) so she would soothe her anxious feelings by saying, "Jean's eight years old, she's old enough to help now." Jean would be given her own key and the responsibility of her brothers and sisters. She tried very hard to take her mother's place, but the job was too much. She had fights with her brothers and sisters and fights with her mother because "You're getting too bossy for your own good!" in the words of her mother. Whenever she tried to get help from her mother, mother was too tired and didn't "... want to come home to all this fuss, — and why didn't you do your homework before I came home?" "Did you fix something to eat?" "Why is this house dirty?" "You been fighting with your brother again?" "Don't talk back to me!" and most likely a cuff for Jean.

THE GHETTO: WHAT IT'S LIKE

Jean's mother was trying to beat the system by making money, because *making money* is the accepted answer, but she was beaten from the start because she could never make enough. One has to have a skill or profession to make an adequate amount of money, and that usually means some kind of formal education, which she did not have. And, because she didn't have this education and money enough to really live, her children were being smashed by the same system.

Teachers may have many children from this type of family background in the classroom, so perhaps we should take a look at the present family situation.

Jean's 18 year old son is a father, but does not see his child and sends no money to the mother because he has none; the 17 year old is a dropout and works at a gas station; the 15 year old is failing in everything, but gym; the 13 year old has just made high school and did well in elementary school and has high hopes; the 11 year old is very slow in reading and doesn't talk too much; the 9 year old is always in trouble and is behind in school; and the 7 year old won't do anything the teacher says. There is nobody in this home to go to for help in school work.

Jean is on Public Aid and home when the children get there, but she doesn't know how to help her children with their homework and doesn't know if it is done correctly or not. So, when she asks, "Have you done your homework?" and the children answer "Yes, can I go out?", she says "Okay, I don't care!" Once they are out of the house, they go where they are fully accepted and they conform to whatever code they must at that time. All they see is what they are already familiar with and school work is the least thing on their minds.

We know that there are many family situations like Jean's but —

(1) The teacher should be careful not to view the entire class as coming from this type of family;

(2) despite the fact that a particular child comes from such a family background, he has a capacity for learning and can develop it. However, with the extreme handicap of such a background, many students without very specialized intensive work, which a teacher may not be able to give, will not be able to make it.

Classrooms, even in the inner-city ghettos, will have numbers of quick-learning students as well as average students, slow students, and dreamers. A teacher may step into a ghetto classroom and find it very difficult to teach because of a feeling that the children cannot be reached. The teacher may become discouraged and develop a sense of hopelessness because of the presence of large numbers of children from homes such as Jean's. Sometimes, however, even in the most deprived situation, there is an aunt, cousin, friend — someone who also is trying to help the student. Perhaps the child is learning through the teacher and that other person, but nothing is evident until two or three teachers later. Through the teacher's work the child will have been helped, and indirectly our society as well.

A teacher may find that students are not acquainted with certain books that he/she was familiar with as a child living in, perhaps, a middle-class environment, but that fact shouldn't leave one with a round mouth and an air of surprise in front of the class. It should be accepted as the fact that it is; and one should go on with the business at hand, that of teaching. A teacher should understand that he/she is a person of importance and influence in the developing life of a child, that each child is an individual, responding individually to the manner in which the teacher does things.

Teachers should be aware of the essential sameness of black and white students, which lies in the fact that they are *all* individuals, reacting to situations in various ways. There will be some students who will react, depending on the situation, in the same way that the teacher will. In other words, any teacher who feels he is facing students whose backgrounds are wholly sub-standard and different from his own, will find it difficult to communicate. In such cases the teacher needs to re-evaluate his conceptions of what constitutes the "difference" which stands between himself and his students. He may find that he is being hindered by stereotyping and prejudices. He may find that by freeing himself of them, he can begin to teach and learn as his students begin to learn and teach.

Up until recent times most black youngsters from poor families could forget about taking certain subjects in school, because mastery of these subjects would not assure them jobs as young adults. They had to face potential employers who could very well be prejudiced, and they had to face the fact of prejudice in the craft unions as well. As a result, they took what jobs they could get. If holding a job interfered with their school work, they dropped out of school, because they believed that "school work" could not solve their problems, and that it was just "kid stuff." Careers that lay open through school, such as medicine, dentistry, and law were much too expensive for most. The talented ones took to music, writing, or sports. If they succeeded, it was all accomplished through hard work. Of course, there were more who failed than succeeded. Today, it would be foolish for a teacher to look at a black student and think with a sigh, "Oh well, they can always sing or run track." Our society seems to be slowly improving with respect to racial relations. With this improvement new opportunities are opening up for those who prepare themselves. We must keep in mind that today's student will be spending most of his working years in the 21st century. Hopefully, by the second millenium, today's racial problems will only be history.

# THREE

# THE GHETTO: HOW IT GROWS

*The persistence of a Black Belt . . . is primarily the result of white people's attitudes toward having Negroes as neighbors . . . formal and informal social controls are used to isolate the latter within congested all-Negro neighborhoods.* — Black Metropolis by St. Clair Drake and Horace Cayton, circa 1945.

On the one hand people profess to wonder why black people live the way they do (or the way it is thought they live) in the neighborhoods to which they have been confined. On the other hand, a question raised persistently, particularly by young white people, is: Why do black people want to move into our neighborhoods?

Reading in newspapers, hearing and seeing on television demands and demonstrations for open occupancy; hearing from their elders about "what happens" when black people move into a neighborhood where they had not before lived, the question is natural and sincere. A neighborhood is very important to most of us, and in our growing years is the place of our most concrete experiences, full of special meanings and personal significance.

The house or apartment in which we live, the block with its sidewalks where we play the "miss or step on the cracks" game; the fireplug we leapfrog over; the mailbox on the corner we lean on when talking with friends; the grocery store, the drug store, the candy store, the lawn where we play mumblety-peg, or the hill where we play king on the mountain; the telephone pole which is base for hide and seek; the school and church we attend; the recreation center, the tavern, and so on, are all parts of our formative experience. As individuals living in a society we are born in a family, grow up in a neighborhood and become members, more or less of a community, city, county, state, and nation. This can be represented by a diagram:

## THE LIFESTYLE OF BLACK PEOPLE

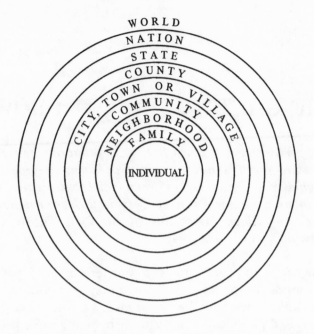

The kind of person we become and our relation to the larger society can be greatly influenced by the neighborhood in which we grow up. Indeed, the neighborhood sometimes is of greater attraction and of greater influence on development than even the family. Delinquents, for instance, are not born, they develop — generally in neighborhoods.

### Seeking Housing

When people reach adulthood and start their own families, they begin looking for a place to live. Probably the one word most commonly used by people to describe where they hope to live is "decent." By this is meant a number of things such as a house or an apartment in good condition, an *un*crowded neighborhood, clean streets and alleys, grass and trees, convenient shopping areas, convenient transportation, good schools, well-behaved neighbors and neighborhood children. People, including blacks, desire a decent place to live.

Blacks, like whites, in looking for housing, try to find the best possible place in terms of decency within their means. As family means increase, people often begin to look for housing they feel will be more adequate to their needs. In other words, people seek to improve their living conditions. If a family moves into a neighborhood, it is because the house or apartment there was available, the family feels it can afford it, the neighborhood is decent and therefore attractive.

The black family who moves into a predominantly white neighborhood is certainly not doing so with the intention of driving whites out of the neighborhood, nor necessarily to "prove" the moral and legal right to live anywhere. On the other hand, the black family certainly is not unaware of what might happen when moving to a "white" neighborhood. The "pioneering" black family realizes that windows might be smashed, that the house might be set on fire or bombed, the children harassed — but hopes these things will not happen. These tactics, violating moral and legal rights, as they do, have nevertheless in many instances succeeded in driving black families from homes they have purchased.

### The Dime and the Quarter

But despite, and because of, illegal and violent efforts to keep blacks out of neighborhoods and confined to a ghetto, the paradoxical situation has arisen of the continued encroachment of black on white areas; of continued expansion of the ghetto and consequent social problems. Black areas in the large cities can be likened to a dime on which the population of, say, the circumference and depth of a quarter, must try to fit. (This dime-quarter analogy was used by the Reverend Jesse Jackson, during the 1966 open-occupancy marches in Chicago). The pattern is that just about anytime those on the "dime" begin to fan out into non-black areas, they find blockades. Their movements are restricted to certain non-black fringe areas, and the inhabitants of these areas react by moving farther away from the black community. The "dime" and "quarter" situation begins anew, merely advancing the hard, clear line of the ghetto.

The expansion of the living area itself is primarily due to sheer population pressure — a result of population growth through in-migration of blacks from the South and a relatively high birth rate among the immigrants. The expansion has taken, and is still taking

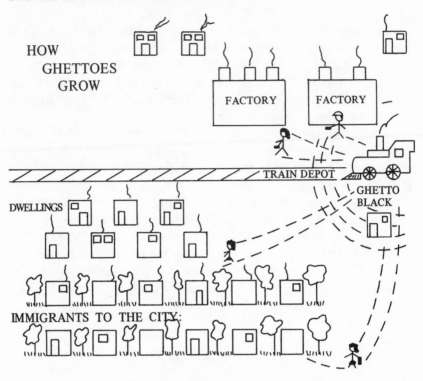

**FIGURE 3—1**
NEW ARRIVALS ARRIVE AND LIVE NEAR THE ENTRY AREA
FIRST WHITE, THEN BLACK EVER MOVING OUTWARD
TOWARDS JOBS AND NEW HOUSES

place in amoeba-like fashion, with the areas fringing the ghetto being engulfed piecemeal. But suppose the expansion of living area for people moving out of the ghetto had taken place on the basis of freedom and right of individual families to choose their residence in accordance with their means, desires, and proximity to their jobs? In that case, black families would be scattered throughout the metropolitan area and our cities would be more desirable and safer places in which to live.

This kind of development, however, was deliberately frustrated. Indeed, in the early decades of this century, black families were driven back into the ghetto from their homes where they had lived for many years in predominantly white neighborhoods.

TYPICAL AMOEBA–LIKE EXPANSION
OF GHETTOES IN LARGE CITIES 1950–70

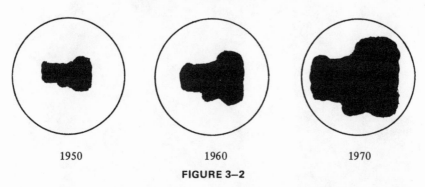

1950          1960          1970

**FIGURE 3–2**

## The Restrictive Covenant

In order to insure that blacks would not move into or re-enter a neighborhood, realtors made use of a device called the "restrictive covenant." A clause was contained in the title to property that the property would not be sold to anyone of the Negro, Oriental, or Indian race. In 1948, The Supreme Court of the United States ruled such covenants to be legally unenforceable. Out-lawing of the restrictive covenant, however, did little to alter the fundamental situation of discrimination in the housing market. Realtors merely refused to show housing for sale and apartments for rent to blacks and others not regarded as white.

## Panic Peddling

Another development arose, and is still booming, facilitating the spread of the ghetto. This has been called "panic peddling" and more descriptively "blockbusting." The process of hemming people in while they are pressing for housing creates a restrictive market which can be manipulated and exploited to the utmost. Profits are to be made from the human misery of overcrowded slums. Large profits are to be made from the transactions of buying housing at a low price from those among whom fear has been sown, and then selling it at a much higher price to those seeking to escape ghetto

49

*A real estate office is being picketed for failing to show houses in white neighborhoods to prospective black buyers.*

(Chicago Sun-Times Photo)

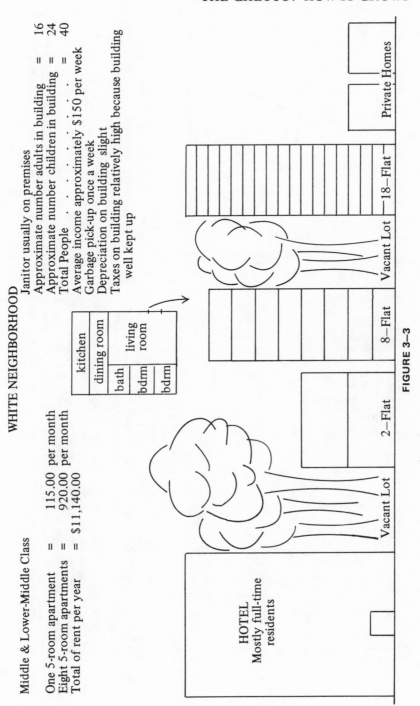

WHITE NEIGHBORHOOD

Middle & Lower-Middle Class

One 5-room apartment = 115.00 per month
Eight 5-room apartments = 920.00 per month
Total of rent per year = $11,140.00

Janitor usually on premises
Approximate number adults in building = 16
Approximate number children in building = 24
Total People = 40
Average income approximately $150 per week
Garbage pick-up once a week
Depreciation on building slight
Taxes on building relatively high because building
well kept up

kitchen
dining room
bath | living room
bdrm
bdrm

Vacant Lot
2—Flat
8—Flat
Vacant Lot
18—Flat
Private Homes

HOTEL
Mostly full-time residents

FIGURE 3-3

51

## CHANGING NEIGHBORHOOD

Rents begin to go up $15 to $20 for white residents, while janitorial services are cut in half. Black residents find out from talking to their white neighbors that they (black residents) are paying much more - - often as much as fifty dollars more - - for the same amount of rooms, in the same condition, and with the same services. If the landlord then asks the white tenant to pay more, the white tenant can simply leave and move to an all-white neighborhood where the rents are lower. The black residents have no choice but to stay and pay the unreasonable rents. The full-time residents of the hotel, upon seeing familiar faces disappearing, move too. The owners of these buildings either sell, or find new and faster ways to make money.

In buildings where no black people yet live, you can see the signs of change. Generally, the owners will stop all services and the building begins to run down. When this happens, the white tenants leave. This is good for the landlord, because the sooner the whites leave, the quicker he can make more money as will be seen on the next page.

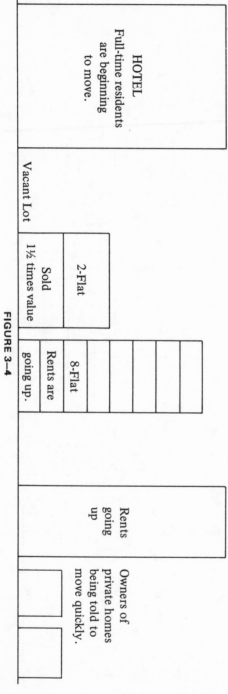

HOTEL
Full-time residents
are beginning
to move.

Vacant Lot

Sold
1½ times value

2-Flat

8-Flat

Rents are
going up.

Rents
going
up

Owners of
private homes
being told to
move quickly.

**FIGURE 3–4**

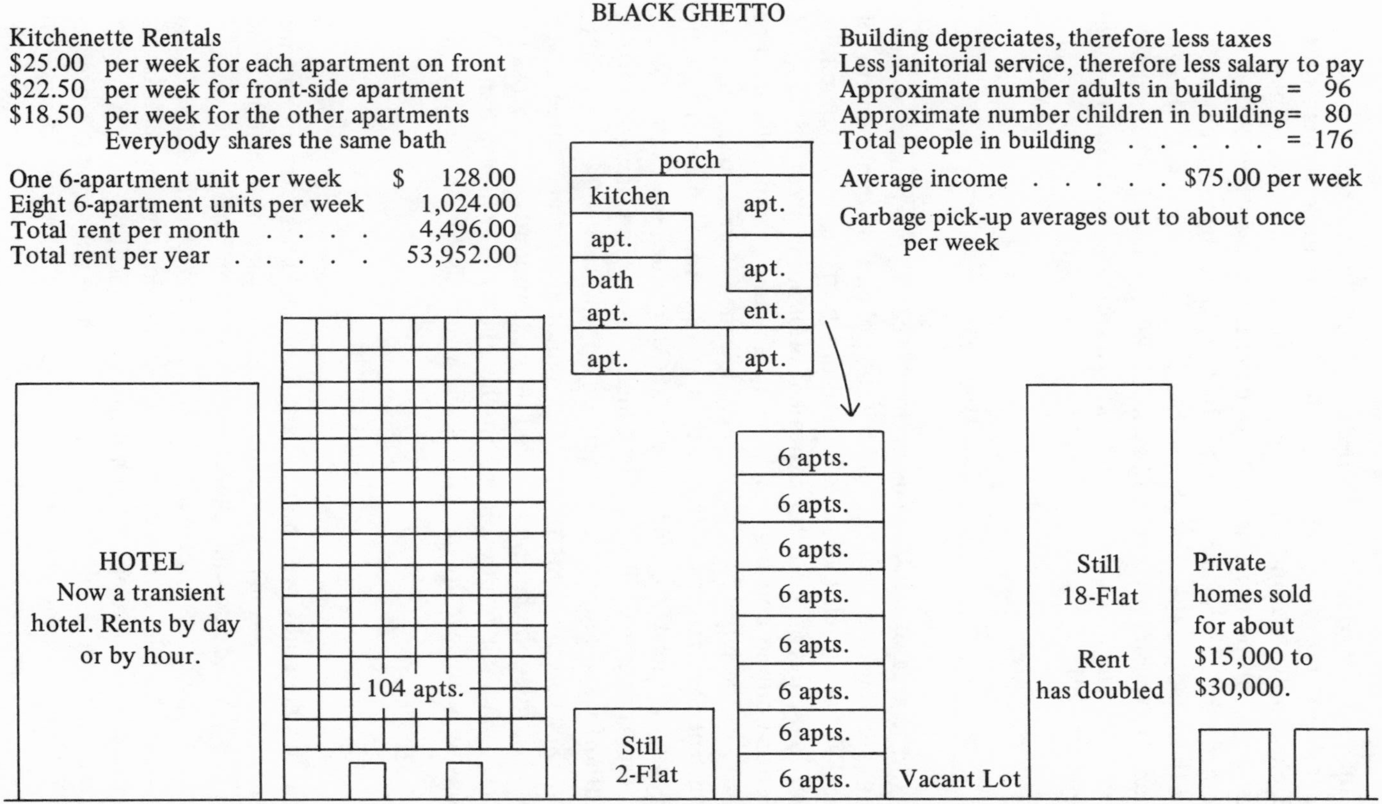
BLACK GHETTO
Kitchenette Rentals
$25.00 per week for each apartment on front
$22.50 per week for front-side apartment
$18.50 per week for the other apartments
Everybody shares the same bath
One 6-apartment unit per week $ 128.00
Eight 6-apartment units per week 1,024.00
Total rent per month . . . . 4,496.00
Total rent per year . . . . . 53,952.00
Building depreciates, therefore less taxes
Less janitorial service, therefore less salary to pay
Approximate number adults in building = 96
Approximate number children in building= 80
Total people in building . . . . . . = 176
Average income . . . . . . $75.00 per week
Garbage pick-up averages out to about once per week
porch
kitchen
apt.
apt.
bath
apt.
apt.
ent.
apt.
apt.
HOTEL
Now a transient hotel. Rents by day or by hour.
104 apts.
Still 2-Flat
6 apts.
6 apts.
6 apts.
6 apts.
6 apts.
6 apts.
6 apts.
6 apts.
Vacant Lot
Still 18-Flat
Rent has doubled
Private homes sold for about $15,000 to $30,000.

**FIGURE 3–5**

slum environs. The "panic peddlers" or "blockbusters" usually operate in areas fringing the ghetto. They circulate rumors that a black family has moved or is moving into an area, that the residents' property values will go down, that they had better sell immediately. They harass people by telephone urging them to sell. By these tactics they are able to buy homes cheaply and then sell them at exorbitant prices to blacks seeking housing. The fact that these practices are illegal in many locations has been of little deterrent effect.

## Public Housing

In the area of public housing for lower income people, we also can see the operation of deliberate policies of confinement of blacks. Forbidden by law to discriminate in the rental of public housing, cities adopted the expedient of building great numbers of highrise public housing units in the already existing ghetto. For years, in the city of Chicago, the Aldermen were allowed to veto construction of any housing in their wards proposed by the public housing authority. In 1969, a Federal Court ruled on a suit brought by the American Civil Liberties Union against the Chicago Housing Authority and ordered this practice stopped. Also, under the ruling, the Chicago Housing Authority is required to place three black families in public housing located in predominantly white areas for every one such family placed in the ghetto — which means the housing will have to be built if the ruling is to be effected.

## White Flight

It has hopefully been made clear, that blacks seek decent housing for the same reasons as everyone else; that they have a moral and legal right to do so, that their rights have been violated by policies of residential confinement implemented through illegal and sometimes violent means. Perhaps it would now be helpful to consider why there exists such implacable hostility; why, failing to prevent a black family from moving into a neighborhood, a process of flight by whites is set in motion as if a plague had struck. Of course, whites, like blacks, have a right to live where they wish, to

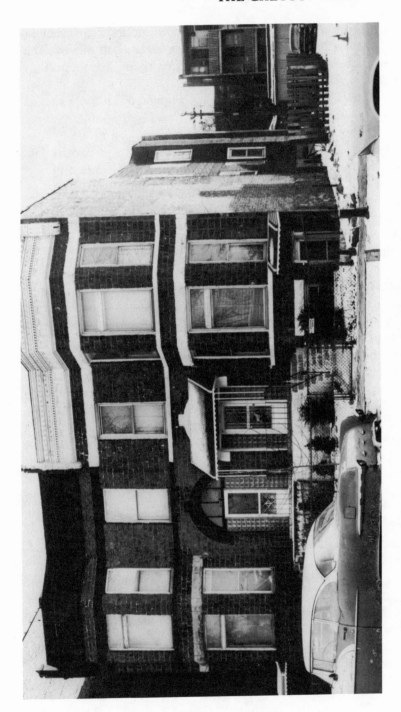

*Home sold by a panic peddler. House was bought by a white for $14,500 and sold a month later to a black for $23,900.* (Chicago Sun-Times Photo)

seek to improve their living conditions, and to define improvement as leaving a neighborhood into which some blacks had moved. The reasoning here seems to be if you cannot fight them, flee them. But, why flee?

About 50 years ago, the following appeared in the Chicago Property Owner's Journal:

> There is nothing in the make-up of a Negro, physically or mentally, which should induce anyone to welcome him as a neighbor. The best of them are unsanitary . . . ruin alone follows in their path. They are as proud as peacocks, but having nothing of the peacock's beauty . . . Niggers are undesirable neighbors and entirely irresponsible and vicious.

Many young people still hear such sentiments expressed by their elders at home and in their neighborhoods; though it is not usual (at least not in the North) for such blatantly prejudicial statements to appear in print.

Probably not all people who flee adhere to anti-human attitudes with the vehemence evidenced in the above quotation. Many people may even doubt that the characterization is altogether true, but the preponderance of their doubt falls on the side of its probable truth. No use waiting around to take a chance. The family down the street has moved. It is probably better to go along with the crowd. A flight hysteria is set in motion.

Now and then we read in the newspapers of families who did not succumb to the hysteria, who elected to stay in their homes when blacks moved in and all other whites fled. These kinds of people report that their neighbors are congenial, friendly, and concerned with upkeep of their property.

Lois Wille, in the March 7, 1970 *Chicago Daily News*, reported on one such family consisting of a father, a mother, and nine children. This family underwent a conversion, finding the stereotypes held by most whites to be distortions. They reported the neighborhood had improved, the blacks keeping up their homes better than the whites who had stopped working on their homes when they felt the neighborhood was going to change. They noted that the adolescent practice of ganging on street corners became a racial stigma in the eyes of whites when it was a matter of black youngsters, though white teenagers had done the same thing.

Well, who is right? The majority who fled, or the few who stayed? Certainly those who fled aren't from Missouri, the type of people who say "show me" and judge by the facts. They grew up in segregated areas and didn't know any blacks. They still do not. Their behavior is of the compulsive type dictated by an obsession compounded by fear and over-generalization. Fear and over-generalizations frequently prevent us from realizing opportunities for new friendships and the expansion of our own human development.

# FOUR

# RELATIONS
# BETWEEN BLACKS AND WHITES

*We shall not always plant while others reap*
*The golden increment of bursting fruit,*
*Not always countenance, abject and mute,*
*That lesser men should hold their brothers cheap . . .*
From the *Dark Tower* by Countee Cullen.

Many white students and teachers (and many blacks too) ask or have on their minds such questions as: Why have the feelings of racial equality and unrest on the part of black people erupted in the last few years? Have relations between whites and blacks improved since the passage of Civil Rights laws, or have they become more strained from the riots, Civil Rights marches, demonstrations, etc.? Do black people dislike white people as a whole? Are black people prejudiced against white people and do they hate them? What can be done to erase white superiority feelings and is anything being done about it? What is the underlying cause of black-white ill-feeling? Could it be the stigma of slavery, identification with an economic class, or fear of things that are different? Let us consider recent race relations history and some of the springs of feeling from which it rose.

Segregation is an evil. Such is the theme of this book. Such have been rulings of the courts. Segregation has been the underlying cause of ill-feelings between blacks and whites. Segregation has constituted a social pattern of behavior the purpose of which has been to strip others of their dignity and self-respect. Segregation has amounted to oppression; and oppressed people, possessed of a sense of dignity, are likely to revolt at some time or another. For who, in Shakespeare's words, will continue to bear the "oppressor's wrong . . . the law's delay, the insolence of office, and the spurns . . . patient merit of the unworthy takes . . . " On the first day of December 1955, a lady in Montgomery, Alabama must have been feeling something like this.

# THE LIFESTYLE OF BLACK PEOPLE

## The Montgomery Improvement Association

On that fateful day, Mrs. Rosa Parks, a seamstress, boarded a bus in Montgomery. She was tired. She had worked all day in a department store and was on her way home. She had suffered segregationist practices all her life, although she considered them wrong and had been secretary to the local branch of the National Association for the Advancement of Colored People. She had taken a seat *just behind* the front section of seats in the bus which were reserved for whites only. The bus filled up. The bus driver ordered Mrs. Parks and three other black people to go further to the rear. By this time all the bus seats were taken and Mrs. Parks would have had to stand in order to make room for a white male who had just boarded the bus. Mrs. Parks refused to give up her seat. She was, in the words of Martin Luther King, Jr.,

> . . . anchored to that seat by the accumulated indignities of days gone by and the boundless aspirations of genera-tions yet unborn. She was the victim of both the forces of history and the forces of destiny. She had been tracked down by the *Zeitgeist* — the spirit of the time.

Mrs. Parks was arrested. She was tried, convicted of breaking the law and fined $10.00 plus $4.00 court costs.

Thus began in the United States what has been called the Negro revolution. Following upon Mrs. Parks' humble but courageous act, the *Montgomery Improvement Association* was formed. The Reverend Doctor Martin Luther King, Jr. was elected its president and he was launched upon his remarkable career for the attainment of dignity and justice — a career ended in 1968 by an assassin's bullet in Memphis, Tennessee, where he had gone to aid garbage workers obtain a decent wage.

The Montgomery Improvement Association organized a mass boycott of the bus system in Montgomery. The association merely asked the city that passengers be seated on a first come first serve basis, that Negro passengers be treated courteously, and that black drivers be hired for routes through predominantly black areas. These requests were denied. Black people were threatened, their homes bombed, the Ku Klux Klan rode, King was convicted of violating an old state anti-boycott law and jailed. In May 1956, while the boycott continued, with blacks going to work in car pools or walking, suit was brought in the Federal District Court to declare segregation on the buses unconstitutional. The court in June so decided, but the city appealed to the United States Supreme Court which on November 13, upheld the lower court. The boycott ended in December 1956, when the Supreme Court mandate reached Montgomery.

## New Definitions

Such was the beginning of an era of racial unrest which has continued up until the present. It was not that dissatisfaction and unrest that were not already there; it was that a moment in history had arrived when the spurns and humiliations burst upon the national, and indeed the international scene, finding focus in an articulate, dedicated and effective leadership. Self-conceptions and definitions began to change, the self-concept of the "new Negro" arose, of the Negro who would not be "turned around" by chicanery, false promises, or a bull-like sheriff with a cattle prod hanging from his belt.

The stigma of slavery has at last been unequivocally rejected on the part of blacks. Their "ill-feelings" are based upon the denial of rights as citizens accorded to them by the constitution and the laws of the land. It probably is true that white ill-feeling toward blacks has a basis in part in the former condition of blacks as slaves. Though particularly true in the South it also is true in the North. This has been true because many children have been told in their homes, with religious sanction, that slavery of a black person was justified because he was black; that blacks were inferior and ordained by God to be servants. Childhood inculcated myths may be hard to shed and color one's judgment negatively even in the face of facts indicating the contrary. Unfortunately, even some churches are still not altogether free of their prejudices. By way of illustration, a parochial school in the Chicago area as late as the 1970's refused admittance to black pupils. The psychological effect of the sanctioned myth has been, in varying degrees, to the effect, how dare he who is inferior assert his claim to equality?

61

## THE LIFESTYLE OF BLACK PEOPLE

It can be said that, on the whole, relations between blacks and whites are different than they were a decade or so ago. It is difficult to say whether they have improved or are more strained. Jim Clark, the Alabama sheriff who made a career of "keeping Negroes in line," often at the head of a posse, felt his relations with blacks were fine. *The New York Times* of February 12, 1965 quotes him as saying "Two hundred niggers live nearer to me than any white person and I have never had any trouble out of them." Certainly, for Jim Clark and others who think like him, the assertion by blacks of their rights as citizens — for instance their right to freely register to vote and to freely cast their vote — are defined as "strained" race relations and a worsening from the time when "niggers" could easily, at will, regardless of their lawful rights, be "kept in their place." The message emanating loud and clear from Montgomery was that black people were no longer "niggers" to be "kept in their place." But let us examine the question further.

"To secure these rights," as our Declaration of Independence states, "governments have been instituted among men." With this rationale the American War of Independence — often called the American Revolution — was launched. The Civil Rights marches and demonstrations begun in the 1950's and continuing through the 1960's were to secure rights to which each and every citizen of the United States is entitled. Speaking of the post-World War I period in the United States, the eminent historian Henry Steele Commager points out:

> There was an open conspiracy, local, state and national, to reduce Negroes and Orientals to the status of second-class citizens, and the violations of the constitutional rights of Negroes in the South were so much the normal thing that when a Negro in that section actually exercised some of the rights guaranteed him by his Constitution it was news.

Commager characterized this phenomenon as "official lawlessness," and it continues to some extent to the present day. The phenonemon was not confined to the South, for Negroes who came to Northern cities "were herded into ghettoes, segregated in most public places, fobbed off with inferior schooling, cold-shouldered by labor unions, and consigned to the most menial jobs," as Samuel Eliot Morrison and Commager state in their book *The Growth of the American Republic.*

## The Sixties' Struggles

About a year and a half before the events in Montgomery, Alabama, the United States Supreme Court made an historic decision affecting the course of black-white relations in this country. The Court held that segregated educational facilities were unconstitutional; and in the following year instructed school districts with segregated facilities to desegregate "with all deliberate speed." The Court held that separate facilities could not be equal and were therefore a denial of equal rights for all citizens. Despite this decision, "official lawlessness" continued. States did not hasten to extend equal rights to blacks on the basis of this decision either in the area of education where it specifically applied, or in other areas of life to which by its nature it generally applied.

This is in marked contrast to what happened after a ruling of the Supreme Court in 1896. At that time, Louisiana had a law requiring black people to ride in separate cars from whites on railroads. Homer Plessy, a black, contested the law on the basis of denial of his rights as a citizen. The Court decided in this case — *Plessy vs. Ferguson* — that so long as the facilities were "equal" they could be separate, and upheld the constitutionality of the Louisiana Law.

Following upon this decision, state after state in the South passed legislation to segregate and discriminate in the area of public transportation and in all areas of life. Separate schools were set up where they had not before existed. Segregation was enforced in hospitals, orphanages, asylums, prisons, cemeteries, etc.; and blacks were systematically removed from the voting rolls. If *Plessy vs. Ferguson* was taken as license to segregate, humiliate and abuse black people, the 1954 decision was not taken as a mandate to desegregate and cease in denial of constitutional rights.

For those who believe in just laws and orderly progress, there can be no doubt that obtaining legal redress is preferable to mass marches and demonstrations. But when confronted with the phenomenon of official lawlessness, of the refusal of governors and

*March on Washington – Demonstrators gather in front of the Lincoln Memorial for a program of speeches by March on Washington leaders during massive civil rights demonstration in August, 1963.* (UPI Photo)

*President Kennedy poses August 28, 1963, at the White House with a group of leaders of the March on Washington. From LEFT: Whitney Young, National Urban League; A. Philip Randolph, AFL–CIO Vice President Dr. Martin Luther King, Christian Leadership Conference President Kennedy John Lewis, student Non-Violent Coordinating Committee Walter Reuther, United Auto Workers Rabbi Joachim Prinz, American Jewish Congress Vice President Johnson, (rear) and Roy Wilkins, NAACP Dr. Eugene P. Blake, National Council of Churches*
(Wide World Photo)

other officials to grant rights even in the face of court orders to do so, what then is the recourse? President John F. Kennedy, proposing legislation in 1963, which resulted in the 1964 Civil Rights Act, pointed out that "in too many parts of the country, wrongs are inflicted upon Negro citizens and there are no remedies at law. Unless the Congress acts, their only remedy is in the street."

The proposing and the passage of the 1964 Civil Rights Act was largely the result of sit-ins in public accommodations, freedom rides, mass protests against segregation and segregation ordinances in Birmingham, Alabama (during which Martin Luther King, Jr. was imprisoned); and the 1963 March on Washington of 250,000 people, 20 percent of whom were white. This Act, which has been called a Magna Charta, provided legal remedies in areas of employment, education, public accommodations, and voting rights. Its most effective provision concerns public accommodations. The desegregation in this area is now of visible and noticeable proportions throughout the country.

Many readers may not remember, know or realize that as late as the early 1960's, on the road between New York and Washington, D.C., people were arrested for asking for service. The situation became one of international embarassment, as even diplomats and officials of foreign countries were refused food, sleeping accommodations, and other public services solely because of their color.

In the area of voting, Congress, in 1965, passed a new and more effective voting rights law; but not before more demonstrations and terrible tragedies. Though there are many unsung heroes in the struggle for human rights and dignity, there are three young men who particularly symbolize the proposition that all men are created equal. Their names should be engraved on our consciousness, never to be forgotten, They are:

James Chaney
Andrew Goodman
Michael Schwerner

The bodies of these three young men, all in their early twenties, were found buried under a dam near Philadelphia, Mississippi. They had been missing 44 days before their bodies were discovered by FBI investigators a few weeks after the enactment of the 1964 Civil Rights Act. James Chaney was from Mississippi and black.

*BOMB VICTIMS — These four Negro girls were killed September 19, 1963 when an explosive, believed to have been a heavy charge of dynamite, was thrown into their Sunday School room at the Sixteenth Street Baptist Church in Birmingham, Alabama. They are, left to right, Carol Denise McNair, 11, Carole Robinson, 14, Addie Mae Collins, 14, and Cynthia Dianne Wesley, 14.*

Andrew Goodman and Michael Schwerner were from New York and white. These young men were part of a student movement to encourage blacks to register for voting in consonance with their legal and constitutional rights.

Though the Supreme Court had made a number of decisions barring segregation of transportation facilities, official lawlessness in this area continued. The freedom rides of the early 1960's were initiated to test and to try to bring about compliance with court decisions in the South. Many of the riders were beaten and imprisoned. A bus was burned in Alabama. (As early as 1947, the Committee on Racial Equality and the Fellowship of Reconciliation initiated a "Journey of Reconciliation" in the upper South to test compliance with a Supreme Court decision outlawing segregation on interstate buses. They met with resistance. Some were imprisoned.)

The 1960's also saw the beginning of what can be called the *Freedom Now* movement in the Northern cities. One of the first

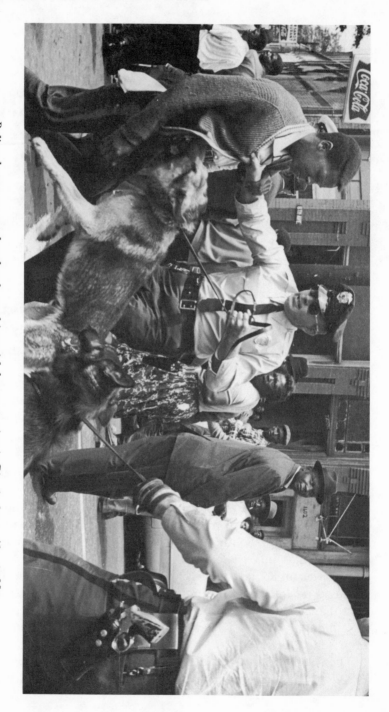

*Police dogs were used to break up this racial demonstration in Birmingham, Ala., in May 1963. Birmingham was one of many U.S. cities, north and south, in which racial violence erupted during 1963, climaxed by the March on Washington in August. (Wide World Photo)*

*Youths trying to cool off are being chased by police during the 1966 Chicago riots.*
(Chicago Sun-Times Photo)

*St. Augustine, Florida:  A motel manager empties contents of jug labelled "muriatic acid" into swimming pool as Negro and white integration demonstrators scream here, June 18, 1964. Over 70 demonstrators showed up at the motor lodge.*                                    (UPI Telephoto)

JAMES EARL CHANEY

MICHAEL HENRY SCHWERNER                    ANDREW GOODMAN

*FBI Circular - Washington: FBI Director, J. Edgar Hoover reported to President Johnson, June 29, 1964 that the search for three missing civil rights workers in Mississippi had been expanded to three states. The FBI distributed thousands of circulars (copy of one shown here) in Mississippi, Alabama, Tennessee, Arkansas and Louisiana.* (UPI Telephoto)

demonstrations was a mass motorcade and march in Chicago to the Republican Party Convention demanding adoption by the Republican Party of a strong Civil Rights platform. Thereafter numerous demonstrations and boycotts occurred with the aim of achieving more and better jobs for black people, integrated quality schools, and an end to enforced residential segregation. These were all peaceful demonstrations designed to secure rights of equal opportunity and protection of the laws. In 1968, Congress enacted open housing legislation, forbidding discrimination in the buying and selling of homes. This was a great step forward. It was in large measure the result of Civil Rights marches led by Martin Luther King, Jr. Though many jobs have been opened to blacks as a result of boycotts and picketing of businesses — particularly those operating within the ghettoes, school and residential segregation still persists.

There can be little doubt that the nonviolent actions of the 1960's on the part of blacks and whites together, whose dedication has

*Fireman sprays water on burning hulk of Greyhound bus which burned on highway just outside Anniston, Alabama after angry mob attacked Negro and white "Freedom Riders" on their arrival to test desegration policies at bus stations in May 1964.* (UPI Telephoto)

been expressed in the song *We Shall Overcome*, were effective in improving the legal, political, and economic status of black people in this country. If nothing else, commitment on the part of the federal government, expressed in legislation, implementing the intent of the 13th, 14th and 15th Amendments to the Constitution was achieved (amendments which were the result of the bloodiest Civil War in history, memorialized at Gettysburg, Pennsylvania where more than 50,000 men were killed in a single battle). This can be considered an improvement in race relations — that is improvement in the status of black people in relation to their government and to the opportunity structure of American society.

## Big City Riots

The opportunity structure of American society leads into consideration of the large scale, dramatic riots of the 1960's in the ghettoes. A great black American poet, the late Langston Hughes, wrote a poem entitled "A Dream Deferred" which says:

What happens to a dream deferred?
does it dry up
like a raisin in the sun?
Or fester like a sore —
And then run?
Does it stink like rotten meat?
Or crust and sugar over —
like a syrupy sweet?
Maybe it just sags
like a heavy load.
Or does it explode?

The riots in the cities during the 1960's represented, in the searing poetic terms of Langston Hughes, explosions of dreams deferred. The ghetto has seen and daily sees in the lives of its people the other aspects, characterized in the poem, of a dream deferred. Like native and foreign-born white immigrants to the cities, blacks came with their dreams of better jobs, better living conditions, freedom from oppression, and more and better opportunities for

*1960 Republican Convention in Chicago*     (Chicago Sun-Times Photo)

*Pickets protest de facto segregation in the Chicago Public Schools in 1960.*
(Chicago Sun-Times Photo)

*Protest riot in Chicago in 1968 which led to ghetto burning and looting.*
(Chicago Sun-Times Photo)

themselves and their children. But for too many dreams instead turned out to be a nightmarish trap — a denial of rights, a crushing of the spirit, a degradation of integrity. The riots were essentially an expression of protest against denial of opportunity and against a white society which continued to maintain barriers preventing participation of blacks in the mainstream of American life.

The non-violent civil rights movement had the effect of raising the aspirations and expectations of black people. There occurred what has been called a revolution of rising expectations. The legal successes in the courts and in the federal legislature served to underline the gap between aspirations and possibilities and the reality of denial of opportunity. Those who participated in the riots were mostly young men. They were in their impressionable years when the mass movements for equality became national news. The *Report of the National Advisory Commission on Civil Disorders*, (Kerner Report), describes a typical participant in the 1967 big city riots as an unmarried Negro male between the ages of 15 and 24. He was likely to be working in a menial or low status unskilled labor job interrupted by frequent periods of unemployment; and felt that he was barred from a better job because of discrimination. He was born in the state and usually was a life-long resident of the city of the riot. He had some high school, and was well informed on political matters. He expressed extreme hostility toward whites, more on the basis of social and economic class than on the basis of race. He was almost equally hostile to middle class blacks.

The riots were acts of desperation with the message to the effect, "This is what we think of the conditions which have been forced on us, and something had better be done about it!" The message also was that blacks were demanding a say in determining their own lot in life. Yet, they were not "race riots" in the sense of race riots earlier in the century, brought about by hostile whites, in which blacks and whites fought and killed each other. They were, in the words of the Kerner Report, disorders involving "Negroes acting against local symbols of white American society, authority and property in Negro neighborhoods — rather than against white persons." Though the riots were the actions of a small minority of the black community, and many black people suffered destruction of their homes and apartments; along with white businessmen and slumlords, they articulated the sense of despair and anger of most of the ghetto population.

## THE LIFESTYLE OF BLACK PEOPLE

Did the riots improve or strain race relations? One thing seems clear; the riots were the outcome of extremely poor race relations, of abuses of black people by merchants, landlords, and the police in particular. There also was too little concern by government and government agencies with the needs and rights of black citizens, of callous disregard by school boards and administrators to the problems of children and their parents.

The aftermath of the riots resulted in greater "strain" between black people and some officials and administrators. The riots helped strengthen a sense of pride and determination among black people, and demands for opportunities and recognition increased. After the riots in the city of Chicago, one of the city's two-year colleges was renamed "Malcolm X" and another "Kennedy-King" by vote of the student bodies. Black men were appointed administrative heads of these colleges. Similar results occurred in other large metropolitan areas. There was increased concern and demands on the part of blacks for a voice in the education of their children. Churches were pressured for greater attention to blacks, and for greater and more responsible black representation in them.

The sense of pride and self-respect among blacks, the surer knowledge that they are as good as anybody else, is a definite gain. There are indications that to some extent racial attitudes of whites have changed for the better, but many whites are still fearful and resentful of blacks moving next door to them, and forcibly oppose blacks entering their neighborhoods. Where they do not succeed with their opposition, they simply continue their exodus out of the city. At the very moment these lines were written, a black family on the Southwest side of Chicago was being continually harassed; the windows of the home they had just purchased were broken and white neighbors interviewed on television expressed indifference to the plight of this family. The head of the family, a workingman, lost time from his job to stay home and protect his family who were determined not to be "run out." There has been no public word of moral support from the city's mayor in this instance nor in the number of other instances where blacks and/or black homes have been attacked. Moral leadership can do much to facilitate the social changes demanded by the times. The desperate kinds of actions by "frightened" whites are certainly not a result of, or reaction to, the ghetto riots. They occurred with regularity long before the riots.

# RELATIONS BETWEEN WHITES AND BLACKS

## Changing Attitudes?

There has undoubtedly been improvement in the attitudes of numbers of employers and of higher educational institutions toward acceptance of blacks as trainees, employees and students. For instance, the Director of the Washburne Trade School in Chicago, a very important institution for training and obtaining jobs in the crafts, reports that in 1966 there were only 112 blacks enrolled (4.6 percent of the enrollment); while in 1973 there were 457 blacks enrolled, comprising 15 percent of the enrollment. (Other minority enrollment increased from 26 in 1966 to 144 in 1973 — a percentage increase of from 1.1 to 4.7 percent.) There are visibly more blacks in a number of occupations from truck drivers to computer programmers and repairmen. Many colleges and universities, both state and private, have sought to increase and have increased black enrollment.

Also, in recent years there have been increasing opportunities for black men to be hired in managerial and executive positions in some large corporations. Many black men now in such positions express concern that they may be only "tokens," whose jobs might be held at the temporary whim of white corporate boards.

This feeling of "tokenism" is reenforced by seemingly condescending attitudes on the part of white executive personnel and board members. They sometimes seem to convey the impression to the blacks that they (the blacks) should exhibit a continual stance of deference and gratitude for being "allowed" to join the corporation, and not be too outspoken. Some black executives, on the other hand, have a feeling that the only reason they have their jobs in the first place is because of violent dissatisfaction expressed in the ghettos during the '60's and the pressures of civil rights organizations. They wish to be reassured that corporate policy toward the hiring of blacks and providing expected job security is not a temporary expedient.

The fact that opportunities have opened and blacks have been able to go into more fields and earn more money represents improvement in race relations. These are gains.

Identification with an economic class has, to some extent, contributed to ill-feeling by whites toward blacks. Ill-feeling by the more affluent toward those in the lower economic classes has been quite common in our cultural heritage. Dickens, in his book *Hard Times*, made a classic statement summarizing this attitude:

> This was one of the fictions of Coketown. Any capitalist there, who had made sixty thousand pounds out of six-pence, always professed to wonder why the sixty thousand nearest Hands didn't each make sixty thousand pounds out of six-pence, and more or less reproached them every one for not accomplishing this little feat. What I did you can do. Why don't you do it?

If the poor express dissatisfaction and take action to better their lot in life, they are accused in the words of Dickens' character, Mr. Bounderby, of wanting "to be set up in a coach of six, and to be fed turtle soup and venison with a golden spoon . . . " For many working people, the hard-won establishment of labor unions has neutralized the ill-effects of this attitude: yet, in large measure, it still persists from the very affluent top of the class structure on down to those somewhat more affluent than the poor. As long as a preponderance of black people are poor, these attitudes are projected on them — just as they were on historical lower classes of England and America — sometimes even by better-off blacks.

But socio-economic class is but one aspect of ill-feelings held by many whites towards blacks. The fact that blacks reach levels of affluence and high accomplishment has not of itself lessened feelings of aversion, rejection, and hostility toward them. When a renowned chemist, Percy Julian, and his family, moved into the Chicago suburb of Oak Park during the 1950's, their home was bombed merely because they were black. The fact that the research of a black physician, Charles Drew, made possible the storage and use of blood plasma which was necessary to save thousands of lives in the second World War, did not result in the desegregation of the Armed Forces or even the desegregation of blood banks. Blood plasma from black and white donors was kept separately during World War II. In 1963, a black banker, Joseph Bertrand, was denied membership in the Catholic Knights of Columbus in Chicago because he was black.

In 1970 the same black banker was slated by the Democratic Party to run for city treasurer of Chicago (and was later elected) on

*Mr. and Mrs. Willie Early show neighbors an epithet which vandals painted on their home under construction in Massapequa, Long Island in 1970. A group of the community's white residents patroled the site nights to keep the vandalism from recurring. The Earlys were the first Negro family to move into the area. With them are, from left: Mrs. and Mr. Richard Shepard and Bruce Hill* (Wide World Photo)

the ticket of the incumbent mayor — a Catholic and a member of the Knights of Columbus. Today, several black families live in the suburb of Oak Park without incident. These developments do reflect a shift in attitudes among some segments of the white population toward acceptance of blacks; and are related to the rise in the socio-economic scale. There are signs that growing numbers of whites are concerned, at least in their consciences, about the injustice of racial discrimination. There are inter-racial groups working toward securing suburban housing for black people. Such activities are facilitated by the existence of federal civil rights legislation — particularly the 1968 legislation forbidding discrimination in the sale of housing. Civil rights legislation in turn is largely due to the emergence of a growing black educated middle-class which has itself been facilitated by fair employment practice policies and legislation of some states and of the federal government. There are a small but growing number of blacks being elected to important political offices with the help of white voters, as well as black. The industrial cities of Gary, Indiana and Cleveland, Ohio have both elected black mayors. It is interesting to note that Carl Stokes, who until 1972 was the Mayor of Cleveland, grew up in a poor family that received public assistance all during his growing years. His brother is now an Ohio Congressman.

The 1973 election of Thomas Bradley as mayor of Los Angeles, with only a 20 percent black population, is another hopeful sign that our society is maturing. The 1973 election of Maynard Jackson as mayor of the first large city in the South, Atlanta, is still another important sign of national maturing. Yet, fear of things that are different, unfortunately, still remains prevalent, expressed most visibly in the form of opposition to integration of schools and neighborhoods. Whites continue to flee in panic proportions from the cities to avoid having black neighbors. They still vociferously oppose having their children attend school with blacks. The ghetto with its high proportion of unemployed, low-paid, and ill-educated workers remains — a monument to fear.

"White superiority feelings" have been responsible for the creation of segregated living. Segregation has created images in our minds of others as being inferior, immoral, unclean, uncouth, etc., and therefore abhorrent. It has also resulted in a degree of oppression. Is it so surprising, then, if those who have been segregated and oppressed, who have experienced hostility directed against them by whites, in turn developed like attitudes toward whites?

Consider for a moment from the autobiography of Malcolm X the following:

> When my mother was pregnant with me, she told me later, a party of Ku Klux Klan riders galloped up to our home in Omaha, Nebraska one night. Surrounding the house, brandishing their shotguns and rifles, they shouted for my father to come out. My mother went to the front door and opened it. Standing where they could see her pregnant condition, she told them she was alone with her three small children, and my father was away, preaching in Milwaukee . . .
> . . . my father . . . had seen four of his six brothers die by violence, three of them killed by white men, including one by lynching. What my father could not know then that of the remaining three, including himself, only one, Uncle Jim, would die in bed of natural causes. Northern white police were later to shoot my Uncle Oscar. And my father was finally himself to die by the white man's hands . . . It was morning when we children at home got the word he was dead. I was six. I can remember a vague commotion, the house filled up with people crying, saying bitterly that the white Black Legion had finally gotten him. My mother was hysterical . . .

Or, consider the following, related by James Baldwin:

> The humiliation did not apply merely to working days, or workers; I was thirteen and was crossing Fifth Avenue on my way to the Forty-Second Street Library, and the cop in the middle of the street muttered as I passed him, "Why don't you niggers stay uptown where you belong?" When I was ten, and didn't look certainly, any older, two policemen amused themselves with me by frisking me, making comic (and terrifying) speculations concerning my ancestry and probable sexual prowess, and for good

measure, leaving me flat on my back in one of Harlem's empty lots.

Try to imagine how you would have felt, acted and developed had you, your parents, kin and/or acquaintances been victims of such wanton cruelty. Would you have fought back? How? Against whom or what? Would you have withdrawn, retreated, tried to escape? How? Would you hate or love your tormentors? Would these emotions become confused in you? Would you learn to discriminate between good white folk and bad "whitey?" Would you overcome? How? If you came to the conclusion that hatred of others rather than love of others was responsible for your plight, how would you convince others to love? If you came to the conclusion that the way society is organized is responsible for your plight, how would you go about changing that society? These are real, hard-core questions that have been and are daily being faced by individuals — including no doubt many readers of this book.

To the questions are blacks prejudiced against whites, and do they hate them just because they are white, the answers can be yes or no; or no and yes. If the questions were asked the other way around; that is, do whites hate or are prejudiced against blacks just because . . . the answers would be the same, would they not? Not all whites hate blacks, or not *all* whites hate *all* blacks. But the main difference between white racism and black is that white racism has been institutionalized. As a result, there have been many grave individual and social consequences. There is a sense in which it is not important whether you dislike me or hate me as an individual. But it *is* very important if your hatred or dislike of me finds expression in social patterns and institutions which deny me a decent job, decent housing in a decent neighborhood, a decent education, etc., because of my color, hair texture, or features. Your freedom should end, to paraphrase an old remark, where my nose begins. As law-abiding citizens we should all be concerned that our laws and institutions provide equal justice and protection. If they do not, social turmoil will occur.

Having been subjected to racism, to hostility directed against them for the mere fact of being black, most blacks probably do not feel an overpowering sense of love toward white people in general. Nor, on the other hand, do most of them feel an overpowering sense of hatred toward whites. But naturally they may have a confusion of emotions — knowing on the one hand that whites are human beings just as anyone else, and on the other knowing of the injustices and cruelties which whites have perpetrated. These feelings have been expressed representatively by an elderly woman living in a black middle-class neighborhood on Chicago's South Side. Her views are to be found in an interview in the book *Division Street: America*, by Studs Terkel. She says:

> I like individual people whether they're black or white or green, according to how they act and how they treat me. How they treat my people . . . I like individuals. But so far as the white race as a whole, no. I don't like them.
> I think there are some that are just wonderful, with their hearts. But they're not enough. They're in the minority, the great minority.
> The majority? That gray old white man — since Washington, not even gray any more — I tell you, I see him as a monster. When I just think about the horrible things that they do, and it's forgotten with the turn of a page. A thousand years from today, if there's another world, if it starts out like America is today, it'll be another hideous mess.
> The white man does not like the Negro and the Negro does not like the white man . . .
> . . . everybody hates. Instead of loving, you hate. I'm speaking of myself, too. I don't have enough love.

This lady admits she has grown bitter, but she has faith and sees things changing for the better. She is proud of her granddaughter who attends an interracial Catholic High School and has white friends:

> The young ones are the ones that are going to change things . . . The young people are not as prejudiced despite the fact that their parents are telling them daily (sic). I'm talking about my own granddaughter. I'm talking about your own children. My granddaughter is not as prejudiced as I am. I want to say that. And I want to say to white

people we Negroes are prejudiced, too. Just like the white
people. We act, and we're just like them . . . But the young
people coming along are going to fool a lot of their fore-
parents. And that's going to be a good thing. Black and
white.

Black people today do not accept the thesis of white superiority,
experience having taught them "whites" are not superior. Further,
in this regard, black people resent continually being the objects of
study and research, of being put in the position of having to explain
that though black they are first human — just as any other racial or
ethnic group.

Know thyself. This is a phrase of good advice most everyone
learns at some time or other. But to know oneself requires self-
examination; and to examine oneself is to ask who, what, and where
am I. This in turn requires a process of what may be called
sympathetic introspection or taking the role of the other — for we
are ourselves only in relation to others, their activities and our
feelings toward others. Attempting to know oneself, and thereby
others, is a first step toward the eradication of ":natural" superiority
feelings. One may ask: to whom am I superior? In what way —
morally, emotionally, biologically, intellectually? How is my
superiority evidenced — by wealth, status, knowledge, power, good
works? In what way am I the equal of or as good as others; or in
what way are others the equal of or as good as I am?

Such questioning can lead to changing self-conceptions. This in
turn can lead to activity directed toward changing those social,
political, and institutional patterns which perpetuate hostility;
those which foster myths rather than truths, those which foster
division rather than unity, those which repress rather than develop
our humanity. Try it. Persist with it. Each of us working together
for a more humane world will ourselves become more human in the
process.

# FIVE

# STEREOTYPES

*Meeting the early tycoons of the music business, Eubie learned what was expected of the Negro: "None of us were supposed to know how to read music . . . If we could read, we had to pretend we couldn't. The day before a show opened we'd get the music. They'd come to the spots after the show and hear us playing the tunes and say: 'aren't they marvellous . . .' "*
They All Played Ragtime by Rudi Blesh and Harriet Janis, Grove Press, 1959. (Eubie Blake was born in 1883. You could count yourself lucky if you chanced to view him on television in 1973, 90 years young, alive and well, playing his piano and sharing his memories with all who would listen.)

Why do blacks usually have luxury cars while their homes are hardly fit to live in; want money but don't want to work; always have a Negro accent? What about the weird body odors all Negroes have? Is it true that blacks have low morals; that rhythm is really innate in the black race and that black boys and girls like only soul music? Do their tastes ever vary? Why do blacks have thick lips and kinky hair? To me all blacks look alike . . . is that true? Why are blacks so good at sports; does the black have a special diet that makes him run fast? If not, how do they do this? Is there emphasis put on self-improvement in the environment of a black child? If not, why not? And a clinching request for a reply which summarizes the underlying theme of all these questions is: Give reasons why Negroes are not inferior to whites.

These kinds of questions are repeatedly asked by young white students from high school through graduate school, as well as by their elders. People working in the helping professions frequently hear such questions or hear them in the form of statements of fact.

There are some sophisticated people who are, or who think they are, free from prejudice who doubt the sincerity of such questions.

They express the view that these kinds of questions are "put-ons"; as if the questioners know better but will not admit it. This may be true, and probably is, in some cases. But these kinds of questions also reflect belief systems which are real, which are determinants of behavior and which are subject in some measure to rational discussion. The trouble is the belief systems have been held by much of the white population without question.

To question is the beginning of dialogue and of doubt as to the validity of assumptions. It can be the beginning of learning by means of unlearning erroneous concepts which constitute prejudice and ignorance rather than knowledge and understanding. Even many older adults who profess belief in equality and equal rights under the law, have such questions on their minds. They may fail to articulate them for fear of being thought to be naive, for fear of themselves being labelled prejudiced, and for fear of the self-knowledge that they too share the belief that blacks are somehow "different," i.e., inferior.

The remainder of this chapter is devoted to discussing the interrelationship of stereotypical views and prejudicial thinking which are manifestly part of our culture. Before proceeding, the reader might like to try the following mental experiment: Review the sample of questions and consider how he has dealt with them on the occasions they have arisen. He should further consider whether and to what extent he has felt limited in forthrightly discussing them, and then attempt to define the conditions which would limit his ability to deal with such questions.

## Prejudice

Prejudice, as is known, runs deep. One would think, for instance, that a university professor of social studies would be free of racial prejudice. His field of study is part of a profession dedicated to scientific observation of mankind; and to date such observation cannot justify the belief that superior traits are the results of color or race. Indeed, the concept of race is one of great imprecision both in the light of historical mixtures of peoples; and because of extreme diversities of physical types, and mental characteristics in any group designated as a race. Yet, such a professor at a prominent university has remarked:

I am white, protestant, a university professor of social studies. I am reasonably intelligent. I believe in the rights of all mankind and I vote a liberal ticket, but personally I still cannot think of any social contacts with blacks on any level. I feel terrible about this . . .

All of us from childhood on carry images in our minds of the world in which we live and the people who populate it. In early childhood our world-mind images contain much of what we later call fantasy. There are, in the child's mind-world, in addition to the real live adults and children close to him, various "little people" such as fairies or leprechauns, good and bad. There are big people capable of gargantuan feats such as Santa Claus or Paul Bunyan. There are various inaminate objects with personalities whom the child talks to or about, such as dolls, toy animals, etc. Even the very young child gives evidence he is aware that he is enjoying a pretend world, but all the same one that is real to him. As the child grows older he learns his images were fantasies which, even though not real, can still be enjoyed in adulthood and passed on for the pleasure and development of the next generation.

The child as he grows is impressionable, and he may, from the adults close to him, "learn" fantasies about actual people whom he will later see and in some manner relate to in the real world. For instance, children in some families not too long ago heard that Jews and Catholics stole small children and killed them in sacrificial rituals. Many children heard in family conversations of the avariciousness, callousness and deviousness of, say, Jews; of the clannishness and the scheming of Catholics to take over the world in a Popish plot. They also heard stories about the stupidity and dissoluteness of Polish people; or of the greasiness, volatility and criminal propensities of the Italian.

The child who heard these things in his family was conditioned, he became prejudiced. As he grew to adulthood and entered the educational and work-a-day world he carried his prejudices with him. But, in large measure, the developing mass, secular, industrial-type society of America, with its democratic ethos, served as a melting pot of these prejudices. People worked and associated with each other and began to learn that their prejudices were false, and that peoples' peculiar trates could actually be appreciated and enjoyed. After a generation or two and the loss of foreign accents,

# THE LIFESTYLE OF BLACK PEOPLE

## STEREOTYPIC LABELING

SHANTY IRISH: An Irishman. A vulgar, offensive term of hostility and contempt; Also: mick, harp and turk.

WOP: Worthless fellow, good-for-nothing; a dark-skinned person of Latin, especially Italian, descent; vulgar term of prejudice and contempt; dago, guines and ginzo.

NIGGER: A Negro. A member of any darkskinned people. A vulgar offensive term of hostility and contempt, as used by Negrophobes. Also: jungle bunny, spade, boot, coon, shine, jigaboo, Zulu, skunk, jig, smoke, snowball.

POLACK: A person of Polish descent; vulgar term of prejudice and contempt. Also: dumb polack.

KIKE: A Jew; vulgar, offensive term of hostility and contempt, as used by anti-semites. Also: sheenie, arab, goose, mockie and yid.

CHINK: A person of Chinese descent; a vulgar, offensive term of hostility and contempt. Also: yellow-belly.

WET-BACK: A Mexican agricultural laborer who illegally enters or is brought into the U.S. to work. An offensive term of contempt. Also greaser.

KRAUT: A person of German descent; an offensive, vulgar term of contempt. Also: dutchie, square head, heinie, pretzel and limberger.

RED-SKIN: A person of American Indian descent; vulgar term of contempt.

BEAD-RATTLER: A Catholic; vulgar term of hostility and contempt. Also: Mackeral-eaters.

SPIC: A Puerto-Rican; vulgar term of prejudice, hostility and contempt. Also: spiggoty.

JAP: A person of Japanese descent; vulgar term of hostility and contempt. Also: skibby.

OTHERS:
CANADIAN: Canucken
CZECH: Bohoe, bohick
ENGLISHMAN: Lime-juicer or limey
FILIPINO: Gu-gu
HUNGARIAN: Bohunk, hunk and hunkie
SCANDINAVIAN: Scowegian, scowoogian, scoovy, sowegian, scandihoovian scandinoovian, squarehead, snooser and herring choker.

AND ON AND ON AND ON AND ON AND ON AND ON AND ON AND ON AND ON AND ON AND ON.

Source: The American Language by H.L. Meneken.

there was no highly visible means of finding the objects of prejudice, unless obviously not white. Intermarriage became common. The political and economic power achieved by ethnic groups helped render ineffective, to a large extent, discriminatory pratices against them.

This is not to say that ethnic prejudices have entirely ceased to exist. Some people of, say, Southern European or Slavic identification feel opportunities are still denied to them because of such identification. Here is how one American of Polish descent has expressed himself only recently:

> I am what you call a PIG (not a policeman). I am a Pole and get the same kinds of treatment as some Italians, Greeks, and Slavs. PIGS. That's the way we're treated. You blacks think you're the only ones discriminated against. Have you ever had to eat lard on bread or take bean sandwiches to school or to work and others laugh at you? You talk about soul food, but I have eaten more ham hocks, neckbones and greens than you have seen.
>
> My father once owned a small grocery store, and one day I fell into a big barrel of "chittlins." The people who bought and ate them were white, and it was a long time before I knew black people called them 'soul food.'
>
> Now let's talk about those jobs you blacks are always complaining about. You holler 'discrimination' if you don't like the way the boss looks at you. Well, what about us, the Poles? Have you heard of the 'dumb pollock' jokes and what that can do to us on our jobs? Some employers believe those jokes and give us the dirtiest, heaviest jobs, because we're supposed to have all our brains in our muscles. I've seen employers promote their kids over better qualified workers or even fire a Pole because they could hire someone else at a lower salary. But I don't see any college kids rushing up to help us PIGS. Where are our civil rights groups?
>
> What about Polish, Italian, Greek or Slav culture and heritage? Do blacks have to learn these histories. In a lot of our blue-collar neighborhoods we need some better schools and teachers, too. But nobody talks about this. If we complain that the blacks are getting everything

and there's nothing for us, we get branded as dumb racists — look at 'All in the Family.' How come the liberals, intellectuals, and politicians don't come and talk and listen to us? There was a time they would talk to the poor and pushed-around masses and try to help, but all they do now is talk to each other and sometimes [the blacks]. We try hard to better ourselves, and it makes me mad when I see you getting more of the pie than you're entitled to. Look at those broken windows in your schools. Do you deny that you people ask, ask and ask and then break up everything in sight when you get it? Are we invisible or something?

To the extent discrimination on the basis of nationality continues to exist, it is regrettable. Many people in the past of various ethnic groups felt compelled to change or modify their names to sound more Anglicized in order to alleviate the pangs of prejudice and discrimination. But for people to change their pigmentations and/or features is hardly feasible. Would it not be better for all of us to feel comfortable in asserting our identities, to join hands in brotherhood, to meet and solve common problems, rather than suffer hostility and division rationalized by stereotypes?

Large numbers of our children and young people, physically segregated, have "learned" (and apparently many still do) in their homes and elsewhere that blacks are morally lax or depraved, childlike, untrustworthy, lazy, always wanting something for nothing, etc. The child is conditioned, prejudiced. He grows up, sees and meets blacks in the real world. He may find something amiss. All the blacks he sees, meets, reads about or sees on television do not conform to the picture. The conscience may become uneasy. But the association is strong — black-bad, threatening. The self as it was conditioned in childhood must be protected.

This is a confusing situation and the thinking goes something like this: "Sure, people are entitled to rights, feel terrible, but must keep distance!" (as in the case of the professor of social studies). "Then there are those others — black, on welfare, illegitimate children, crime in the streets, want to move into white neighborhoods; fearful, threatening, let them stay where they are, improve themselves, become human — like me." There's the rub, "human like me." Lillian Smith, in her book *Killers of the Dream* tells a parable about a bargain between Mr. Rich White and Mr. Poor White which goes, in part, like this:

> Always the Negro was somebody who took things away, scraps and taxes, prestige, shoddy and second-hand things, but things away from you. Always he was something you had to prove you were better than, and you couldn't prove it. And always he was something you had to hate and be afraid of. It was something like this: If he wasn't human like you said, if he wasn't, you'd never know what he might do, you couldn't count on him; he might do all the things you had wanted to do or dreamed about doing that you knew were not human, all the kinds of things you know other folks would want to do if they were not human. And sometimes it was like this: If you let yourself believe he is human, then you'd have to admit you'd done things to him you can't admit you've done to a human.

If one has grown up, imbued in childhood with the belief in the inferiority of blacks and the necessary converse, one's own superiority, it can be very difficult to acknowledge that blacks are actually, or even can be, one's equal as a human. Evidence that blacks are equally human is suppressed. What can be called a split in the self occurs. One of the reasons for this is that as we grow up we learn something of the principles of democracy which embody the concepts of dignity and equality. These are in conflict with the earlier conditioned self holding that blacks are in fact inferior and not equal. Undesirable behavior, prevalent throughout society, is associated with blacks; and fear or abhorrence of such behavior is displaced upon black people. They become the biblical scapegoat — the object upon which the sins of the whole people are placed and offered for atonement. (See Leviticus, Chapter 12:7-10).

### Their Morals and Ours

Many Blacks know, and have known, that they are not inferior to whites, and still more are coming to realize and to assert this. They have had long years of experience in observing and being the objects of the behavior of whites in various classes of our society. They have learned that their behavior as blacks does not suffer in comparison with the behavior of whites. Black people, in the face of great adversity, have and do exhibit what are generally considered moral virtues such as patience, humility, courage, fortitude, diligence, helpfulness, compassion, tolerance, kindliness, frankness, integrity, loyalty, honesty, etc. Though this too is stereotyping, it has about as much validity as the opposite stereotype of blacks as lacking in morality and ambition.

Blacks indeed have low morals, but so do whites. However, on any measure of violence or brutality toward or degradation of other men — white, black, brown, or whatever — the so-called white race cannot be surpassed. Elijah Muhammed, the leader of the Black Muslims in the United States, calls the white man "the Devil," on the basis of the crimes against humanity which have been committed by "white men." They have committed every conceivable crime from individual murderous rape to genocide against peoples of all colors and creeds including people belonging to their own race. (Black men in various parts of the world and at various times have behaved similarly.) Does any white reader of whatever national or linguistic heritage wish to claim Adolph Hitler or Adolph Eichmann? (The latter executed by the State of Israel for his role in sending Jews to extermination camps). No one has yet made out a case that they were black. Certainly blacks do not wish to claim them as part of either their biological or cultural heritage.

Sexual morality of black people is generally a concern of questioners, usually centered around illegitimate children and prostitution. All readers of magazines and newspapers cannot help but be aware of the changing sexual mores in our country. Many college and university students are themselves involved in such changes as unrestricted visiting in dormitories of the opposite sex or co-ed dormitories. There has been in recent years increasing clamor for repeal of laws prohibiting abortions. Many states have passed laws making it a relatively simple matter for a woman, married or unmarried, to obtain an abortion. The United States Supreme Court has now held unconstitutional laws prohibiting abortion. All this has been done without any significant help or clamor from the black population.

The cases we read about in magazines and newspapers, see and hear about on television regarding the obtaining of abortions, or of getting abortions under the liberalized laws, typically involve young, unmarried white women of fairly good education. They are not ignorant of birth control methods. Lois Wille, in the *Chicago Daily News*, January 30, 1971, cites the case of Sally, who went to New York for a legal and relatively cheap abortion. Sally and her boyfriend were both from well-to-do Chicago suburban families. Sally did not use birth control pills, claiming they made her ill. Her boyfriend felt that other precautionàry measures which could be used to prevent pregnancy were a hindrance to full sexual enjoyment. When Sally became pregnant, neither she nor her boyfriend were willing to accept the responsibility of having a child. The "Sallys" of our country number in the several tens of thousands yearly.

Unmarried pregnant women typically find themselves faced with questions of what to do about their pregnancies. Should they have an abortion? Should they deliver the child and keep it? Should they deliver the child and give it up immediately for adoption? The adoption agencies of our country have been kept quite busy for the past three generations finding homes for children of unmarried white women. Physicians willing to risk the penalties of the law, have become wealthy performing abortions upon white women who could afford to pay the price, and felt unable to undergo the ordeal and perhaps stigma of bearing an out-of-wedlock child. It would seem comparatively few white women have kept their babies conceived "illegitimately."

Black women, like white women, become pregnant while unmarried. They are faced with the same questions of what to do about their pregnancies. Although faced with the same questions, black women in large numbers have not had the same alternatives available to them. Adoption agencies, until relatively recently, were essentially for whites only — one of the reasons for this being that there was little demand from childless couples to adopt black children. To arrange for an abortion in the case of an undesired pregnancy (even a medically unsafe one) requires a certain level of sophistication and "connections" not generally possessed by black women in the lower socio-economic levels who give birth to most out-of-wedlock children. Among the black middle-classes, illegitimate birth rates are comparatively low and no higher than among the white middle classes.

Prostitution exists because there is a market for it — at all levels of society. The $100 and more call-girls we typically read and hear about are not black, though there are no doubt black prostitutes on this level. In poverty-stricken areas the world over, street-walkers are numerous. This likewise is true of the black ghettos in the United States. A young student from Gary, Indiana asked, "Why do more black girls in Gary take to prostitution than do white girls?" Poverty, price and market demand explain it. Girls in the poor ghetto areas cater to white "johns" who come into the area seeking sex relations as well as to the black men. They frequently charge more affordable prices than white girls simply because of the poverty area in which they find themselves.

Much prostitution is by women — black and white — who are addicted to narcotics. It is a way of earning money to support the addiction which is very expensive. In some areas of the black ghettos rates of drug addiction are very high. This drug addiction (including alcoholism) is frequently rooted in hopelessness and despair generated by racism. Society reaps what it sows. Other girls and women engage in prostitution from time to time to make ends meet when there is little or no money coming in due to lack of employment. There are some, no doubt, who are prostitutes simply because they find that way of life exciting and fairly remunerative.

## Reality and the Stereotypes

The great American psychologist and philosopher, William James, wrote about what he called "the will to believe," and about a "certain blindness" in human beings. Both of these characteristics of human behavior can operate very powerfully to the extent that people neither believe what they see (or hear), nor see (or hear) what is contrary to their belief. This psychological selectivity embodied in the stereotyped views we hold of others, can have negative and harmful effects.

It has happened that black people seeking employment, for which they were qualified, have made telephone appointments for job interviews. Upon arriving for the interview, they have been confronted with somewhat startled, embarrassed personnel interviewers. The results of the interviews were to the effect: "Well, yes, but we have quite a few applicants for the job, you understand. We'll see. We'll call you in a few days to let you know." A few days pass and the black applicant has had no word from the employer, so he calls and is told, "Sorry, the job has been filled." The point here, of course, is that when the interview was arranged over the phone, the person on the employer end of the line did not know the caller was black. He therefore, signalled encouragement. Blacks are supposed to have a "Negro" accent. Not detecting it throws a "monkey wrench into the works" for the "listening" white person on the employer end of the line. Moreover, it is much more frustrating and annoying to discourage a black looking for a job while looking him in the eye.

White salespeople have arranged appointments with black women in or around integrated or transitional neighborhoods. Upon arriving at the home, the door being opened by a black woman, the salesperson asks if the lady of the house is in — assuming that the black woman must be the maid or housekeeper. Such incidents are the basis of somewhat bitter humor among black people.

The fact is, there is no one "Negro" accent, and all blacks do not sound alike. There are in this country various regional accents and styles of speech. Black peoples' accents and speech styles generally approximate the regional norm of the area in which they grew up. There are exceptions to this. For instance, many black people from the deep South have no noticeable drawl or slurring of speech, such as is characteristic of white Southerners. Their accents are closer to those of white Northerners. In the Northern big city ghettos, there is a style of speech black people sometimes refer to as "street talk." It is largely monosyllabic, ungrammatical English, which is as much mumbled as spoken. Many black parents are concerned that this language pattern picked up by their children in the street does not become habitual. They emphasize to their children the importance of learning to speak correct and standard English.

On the other hand, there is a rhyming, creative type of English which has a tradition, particularly among young black men, composed of phrases such as: "Hey, man, shake my han'." "Say, baby, I'm a poet, you better know it, 'cause I'm about to blow it!"

# THE LIFESTYLE OF BLACK PEOPLE

"Hey, man, where ya been, I just got back, ya better gimme some skin!"

It is somewhat amazing that in this age of mass media, affording exposure to black news commentators, actors, entertainers, athletes, political and social leaders, that people, particularly young people, continue to maintain that all blacks sound alike. But such is the power of belief in stereotypes.

Many young people, yet today in this age of random and colorful fashions, ask about what they have learned to call "nigger colors." In their conception, bright colors — oranges, yellows, reds, greens, purples, and combinations of these colors — are associated with the characteristic dress of black people. Only the ability of the stereotype to distort perception can account for the idea that blacks in particular have an affinity to such colors in modern times. Black men and women, just as white men and women, are style conscious; and both generally have the same styles from which to choose. Today bright colors are "in" and are attractive.

A young white woman, a graduate student in education, enrolled in a course on race relations, was taken to a meeting in Chicago of Operation Breadbasket. (Operation Breadbasket was a Northern arm of the Southern Christian Leadership Conference, and was concerned with obtaining more and better jobs for the black and poor people; using, if necessary, picketing and economic boycott. In Chicago, under the Reverend Jesse Jackson, informational and inspirational meetings were held each Saturday morning attended by several hundreds of blacks, well interspersed with brown and white people joining them. Late in 1971, the most influential leaders left to form Operation PUSH — People United to Save Humanity devoted to the same goals.) On the way to the meeting, the young woman commented that black people wear different colors than white people. She was convinced of this, though her association with blacks had been practically nil. She was asked upon arrival at the meeting, to observe as much and as carefully as she could the dress of the hundreds of black people there. She had to admit, with the reluctance of one giving up a cherished notion, that the dress of the black people in the large assembly was what the dress of whites would be. Some bright colors were there, but no more than in any other audience without uniforms would be.

However, less than two hours later after leaving the meeting she firmly reiterated her former statement that "Black people do wear different colors than whites!" and "Anyway, the people in the meeting at Operation Breadbasket were just different."

The idea that black people are particularly prone to owning Cadillacs or other luxury automobiles, while they live in hovels, is by now an ancient, but apparently tenacious, stereotype. While it is true that some black people own luxury cars, it is probably safe to add that many of those who do own them can afford them and do not live in hovels. In some instances it is true, blacks of modest means spend larger proportions of their incomes on fancy automobiles rather than on housing; which in part can be explained by the limited availability to blacks of decent housing.

Blacks, like whites, upon reaching levels of relative affluence, acquire goods considered to provide greater quality and comfort; and which serve as symbols of economic and social status. Many black doctors, businessmen, politicians, lawyers and other highly paid professional people do buy luxury automobiles. Black social workers, teachers, salespeople, bus-drivers, technicians, clerks, etc. usually buy the more modestly priced automobiles — many of them opting for the relatively inexpensive smaller foreign imports.

Among the poor, low-paid classes of blacks, just as among poorer whites, used-cars of various vintages and styles are the rule for those venturesome enough to purchase a car. They are often the victims of unscrupulous dealers and finance companies who solicit their trade, sell them over-priced cars, repossessing the cars when payments fall behind, reselling them to other victims, while exacting payment from the original purchasers as well. Because one observes a group of not-too-well-off white people gaily riding about town in a second-hand Cadillac convertible, one would not conclude that all whites have luxury cars while living in poorly maintained homes. Could not this same fairness of thought be directed to black occupants riding in a second-hand Cadillac?

Not long ago, even in northern industrial cities, one rarely saw black people in such occupations, as truck drivers and deliverymen (milk, bakery goods, beverages, etc.), telephone linemen or repairmen, auto mechanics, clerks or managers in chain grocery stores, large department store salespeople, bank clerks and officers, sales representatives, secretaries, laboratory and medical technicians. Today, blacks may be seen working in these and many other occupations that once were closed to them.

PERCENTAGE OF FAMILIES
RECEIVING AID TO DEPENDENT CHILDREN BY RACE

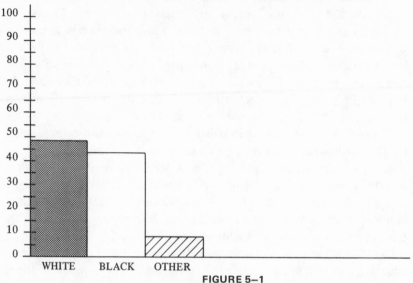

**FIGURE 5–1**

Source: DEPT. OF HEALTH, EDUCATION & WELFARE, WASH., D.C. 1972

Certainly, the fact that black people are now found working at a variety of jobs is no indication that they want money, *but* are unwilling to work for it. Nor were these jobs easily come by. There have been years of struggle through legal, political, morally persuasive and direct action (e.g., demonstrations and boycotts) against discriminatory and exclusionary hiring policies which barred blacks from many occupations. Today, black men are making efforts to be hired in the construction trades. They are meeting resistance from the membership of many of the union organizations in the construction field. Yet, the same people who have and do oppose the possibility of blacks being able to work at jobs providing a decent income say with assurance that the trouble with blacks is that they want money, but don't want to work for it.

The stereotype that black people do not want to work is associated in the white popular mind with black people receiving public financial aid — and they (the whites) do not see why they have to pay taxes to support blacks "who do not want to work." In

**100**

MYTH:

The welfare rolls are full of able-bodied loafers.

FACT:

Less than one percent of welfare recipients are able-bodied unemployed males: some 126,000 of the more than 13.6 million Americans on Federal/State-supported welfare (October 1971 statistics). All these individuals are required by law to sign up for work or work training in order to continue to be eligible for benefits. Prior to enactment of the new work-training law, government studies in three cities (Los Angeles, Milwaukee, and Camden) indicated that 80 percent of the able-bodied unemployed males on welfare did want to work. Nationally, among the fathers in this group, one in three was already enrolled in work training.

The largest group of working-age adults on welfare are 2.5 million mothers of welfare families, most of whom head families with no able-bodied male present. About 15 percent of these mothers work, and 7 percent are in work training. Many of the other mothers confront serious barriers to employment under the existing welfare system, such as lack of child care facilities, transportation, etc. With additional day care service and job training available, it is estimated that another 34 percent would be potential employees. About 4 percent of welfare mothers require extensive social and rehabilitative services to prepare them for employment.

The remaining 40 percent have little or no employment potential because they care for small children at home, have major physical or mental incapacities, or other insurmountable work barriers.

**FEDERALLY ASSISTED WELFARE POPULATION**
**(as of October 1971)**

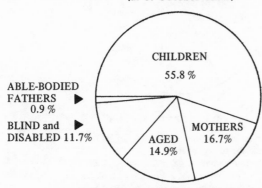

ABLE-BODIED
FATHERS ▶
0.9 %

BLIND and ▶
DISABLED 11.7%

CHILDREN
55.8 %

AGED
14.9%

MOTHERS
16.7%

**Factors in the Employability of Welfare Mothers**
**(From a 1969 study)**

* Needed at home to care for small children, have a long-term disability, etc. . . 40%
* Employable if job training, jobs, and day care were made available . . . . 34%
* Already employed full or part-time . . . . . . . . . . . . . . 15%
* In work-training programs or waiting to be accepted . . . . . . . 7%
* Need extensive medical or rehabilitative services before becoming employable . 4%

**FIGURE 5–2**

Source: DEPT. HEALTH, EDUCATION & WELFARE, WASH., D.C. 1972

# THE LIFESTYLE OF BLACK PEOPLE

## MYTH:

Once on welfare, always on welfare.

## FACT:

Half the families on welfare have been receiving assistance for 20 months or less. Two-thirds of families have been on the rolls less than three years. About one in five families (17.7%) have been on welfare for five years or more, and about one in 16 families (6.1%) have been on the rolls ten years or more.

Current figures show that about 65 percent of cases are on welfare for the first time; about one-third of cases have been on the rolls before.

Proposed welfare reforms are designed to strengthen work incentives, eliminate barriers to employment, and thus help present recipients rejoin the work force as soon as possible.

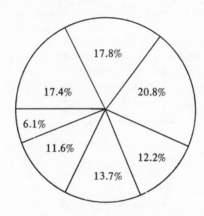

**Length of Time on Welfare**

| | |
|---|---|
| Less than six months | . . . . . 17.4% |
| Six months to one year . | . . . . 17.8% |
| One to two years. | . . . . . 20.8% |
| Two to three years . | . . . . . 12.2% |
| Three to five years | . . . . . 13.7% |
| Five to ten years . | . . . . . 11.6% |
| Ten years or more | . . . . . 6.1% |

**FIGURE 5—3**

Source: DEPT. HEALTH, EDUCATION & WELFARE, WASH., D.C. 1972

the white popular stereotype, it seems also to be assumed that most of the people on public aid are black. In certain highly concentrated urban areas, where blacks have migrated, primarily in search of job opportunities, this is true. But two things need to be said about this. Black working and entrepreneurial men and women pay taxes for the support of social services (and war) and public aid as do whites. The majority of people in receipt of public aid (about 58 percent in 1970) are white, nationwide. Of the over 2 million families with their more than 6 million children receiving money through the Aid to Families with Dependent Children program, almost half the families and children are white, and somewhat less than half are black.

Nevertheless, despite advances made by blacks in securing jobs in various areas, unemployment, underemployment, and large numbers on welfare are widespread in the black ghettos. In part, this is due to lack of education and training in skills from which blacks have been more or less deliberately excluded by our society. Leon H. Sullivan, a black minister, relates (in his book *Build Brother Build*, McCrae Smith, Philadelphia, 1969) that after blacks had obtained the kinds of jobs they had never before held in Philadelphia as a result of Selective Patronage (consumer boycotts by blacks against certain companies):

> . . . a new kind of problem emerged. Our people were getting jobs, but it was becoming more and more difficult to find people to fill some of the jobs. There were jobs that black people had never had the opportunity to hold before in sizeable numbers. Hundreds of good jobs that the white man had always kept to himself became available overnight: . . . jobs that we had always hoped for but only a few of us could ever get before. And for most of these jobs high accuracy was an absolute necessity.

Since companies and the government were not providing the types of training that prepared trainees for actually existing jobs they were guaranteed to get, the Reverend Sullivan founded a program called Opportunities Industrialization Center (OIC) to train young ghetto men and women in needed job skills. He secured the cooperation of several large companies who provided

Blacks and Chicanos demonstrate in 1971 for the right to work on construction jobs. (Chicago-Sun Times Photo)

equipment for training and guaranteed jobs for the trainees. The program has been quite successful in Philadelphia and has been instituted in other cities across the nation. Reverend Sullivan himself has recently acquired a new, or added, position. In early 1971 he was named to the board of directors of the General Motors Corporation. He is the first black man to sit on the board of such a large corporation in the United States.

The presence of black people in various jobs from which they were before excluded and the emergence on the national scene of numbers of blacks of prominence and achievement indicates there has been a good deal of emphasis on self-improvement among black people. One can rest assured that in the homes of such black people, there is much emphasis on self-improvement of their children. It is true that there are many homes in the ghettos where the child receives little in the way of encouragement or training in developing perceptual, motor, and language skills. These children are often, but not necessarily, from broken homes. Even in homes where the parent or parents emphasize learning and good behavior habits, the environment of a deteriorated neighborhood with its high deliquency rates can be a greater attraction and influence on a child than the home.

Many children in the ghettos have parents who are themselves poorly educated (many from the "deep south" where they were deliberately not educated), and are not equipped to provide the type of educational stimulation required for urban living. Nevertheless, poor black parents, just as white middle-class parents, expect the school system to educate their children; to prepare them so they will be able to get good jobs. Many black parents, including many poor ones, are sure that the public school systems of the urban areas have short-changed their children. This is more than enough reason for vigorous demands by black parents for community control of schools in black neighborhoods. Black people are aware that the slum environment in which they are contained by deliberate policy is not the best for their children. They hope for and endeavor to achieve their children's improvement against great odds.

Many school children in the ghettos, it is true, have perceptual and learning difficulties. A ghetto child may have difficulty in distinguishing, say, the capital letter K from R, of C from G, of E from F, of B from D, or O from Q. If the child were given a list of the ten letters B D E F G K O Q R and asked what one thing must be done to five of the letters in the series to make them look similar to five *other* letters in the series, it might take him a while to comprehend. But the white young person in high school or college or the white adult must also be suffering from similar perceptual and learning difficulties if he maintains that all black people look alike or professes to be unable to tell the difference between the appearance of one black person and another.

Probably most people in this country identified as black have "kinky" hair, although a great many of them do not. Up until recent times, most black women and many men kept their hair straightened and coiffured in various styles. Therefore, to any objective observer, "kinky" hair could not be a criterion for all blacks looking alike. On the other hand, most black people, when the question arose, stated that white people had "straight" hair. When the "natural" hair fashion look came into being, blacks were surprised and later amused to discover that they had not been the only ones using hair straighteners. Many of them, perhaps for the first time, saw white people wearing their hair in its naturally kinky state, whether the hair color was blonde, red, brown, or black even though most white people do have naturally straight hair.

As to "thick lips," fullness of lips among black people with "kinky" hair varies tremendously — some having quite thin lips. Even if we observe only those black people with their natural (kinky) hair and "thick lips," there are among this group so many differences of physique, physiognomy, and shades of brown skin color as to defy classification. It is gross perceptual error to conclude from the characteristics of kinky hair, thick or full lips, and brown skin that all black people look alike. But such is the power of the stereotype and the will to believe in it. The stereotype, blinding perception, is the product on the one hand of segregated living and on the other provides a reason for keeping people apart. It would seem, for instance, that the school systems of this country have a marvelous opportunity to educate children on the full range of human types within and between races using various paintings, photographs, and other media, along with discussions on similarities and differences. And in high school it would seem that students should get good grounding in laws of genetic transmission insofar as these are known.

Many years ago advertisements for *Lifebuoy* soap started using an abbreviation which has since become a household word. Everybody knows what is meant by, and at one time or another uses, the term "BO" (body odor). It is now listed in Webster's Dictionary. *Lifebuoy* ads used to make a pitch particularly to young people through its ads. The ads (often included in the newspapers' comic section) would tell the story of a young adult who could not keep a girl or boyfriend until someone brave enough came along to tell the young person that his or her trouble was BO! All one had to do was to take a bath using *Lifebuoy* soap and the human relations problem would be solved.

Today, mouth washes and other deodorant products are marketed in this manner on television. Blacks, like whites, have long been exposed to the use of soap for basic cleanliness and to the various deodorant and scent products for masking odors which can result from natural body secretions. Soap and "smell good" products enjoy a large market among the black population. It is very doubtful that any larger proportion of blacks than whites is afflicted with "weird body odor." But just as in the old BO ads, who wants to associate with anyone who has BO? The stereotype that all blacks smell bad is just another myth justifying disregard for fellow human beings and rationalizing prejudice.

One of the biggest advertisers of soaps, deodorants and other kinds of "smell-good" products is *Ebony* magazine which is aimed at the black middle class consumer. *Ebony* was founded by John H. Johnson in 1945. His might be considered a typical American "rags to riches" story. With money borrowed by his mother on her furniture, in the sum of $500, he started in the publishing business. His large and very successful publishing company now has its headquarters in a multi-million dollar building on Chicago's famed Michigan Avenue.

A black writer, Ronald L. Fair, wrote a novel, entitled *Many Thousands Gone* (Victor Gollancz, London 1965) about race relations in the South based in part upon a true incident involving *Ebony* magazine.

White people in certain parts of the South tried to prevent black people from receiving the magazine; and they (the whites) would not believe that blacks in the North lived as well as depicted in the magazine. "It was not healthy," in words from the novel, "to go around saying the Negroes in the north lived better than many whites in the south."

"All God's Children Got Rhythm," as an old song says. This can be translated as rhythm is innate in the human race. Whites have rhythm and so do blacks. It is very doubtful that rhythm is more "innate" in one racial group than another though rhythmic expression in its form, complexity, and pervasiveness may vary from group to group and time to time.

In Memphis, Tennessee, there is a statue of W.C. Handy (composer of "St. Louis Woman"), a black musician often called the father of the blues as he is reputed to be the first one to formally compose blues. Blues, jazz and spirituals are acknowledged American contributions to the world's musical culture. And this music is indelibly associated with the black man in America. Rhythmic patterns basic to the origin of the jazz-blues art form are a part of African heritage which was not altogether lost by black people brought to this country as slaves.

Rhythmic, swinging music became a part of, and was passed on as, a heritage through the Christian worship services of black people. There has been and there is a great deal of musical talent found among black people. Expression of this talent is not limited to jazz and "soul" music. There are popular composers, serious composers, and grand opera performers as well as outstanding instrumentalists. There are many popular songs enjoyed and sung or whistled by the last couple of generations of white people, probably most of whom were unaware that the composers were black. For instance, Eubie Blake and Noble Sissle composed "I'm Just Wild About Harry", Shelton Brooks wrote "Some of These Days," and "Dark Town Strutters' Ball", Fats Waller and Andy Razaf wrote "Honeysuckle Rose", "Ain't Misbehavin' " and "Keepin' Out of Mischief." The ever popular "Solitude", "Mood Indigo", and "Sophisticated Lady" were composed by Duke Ellington.

Not all black people, however, are possessed of musical and rhythmic abilities. If rhythm is "innate" in all black folks, there are certainly many who have been unable to develop these gifts. At parties of black young people, just as at white young people's parties, there are dancing "duffers" and wallflowers. To ask if black young people dig "soul music" only, is like asking if white young people only dig rock. Rock and soul music have been very popular among youth. There is a great deal of rhythmic rock music produced and performed by black musicians, and marketed in black areas. It reflects the cadence and flavor of life in the big-city black ghettos — it is soul music and good dancing music. It also is a source of pride in the achievements of the soul brother who produced it. Many white young people enjoy soul music as well as other musical styles. Many black youngsters also enjoy other musical styles, including country, western, popular, and classical music. There are even black country and western music performers. It certainly is true that black young peoples' tastes vary; but they are going to do their own "thing" and let all the world know that black and soul music are great.

Some people, black and white, seem to have a natural ability for sports. All those who have this ability do not pursue active sports participation with the same degree of intensity or dedication, or seek a career in this area. Besides having basic ability, athletes have to practice continuously and keep in training through exercises and proper dieting. Size and weight can be decisive factors depending on the sport. In addition, athletes must have a will to compete and win, and in team sports, a team spirit. Finally, athletes must have the opportunity to be accepted into the arena of organized sports if they are to achieve prominence, prestige and financial reward.

Baseball is now integrated. Black baseball players are named year after year as most valuable players. But until 1947, when Jackie Robinson was brought into major league baseball, blacks were excluded from the big leagues. Top athletes who are black are now found in most major sports. Track, which is still considered an amateur sport, has long had top black performers. For years black athletes have won for the United States in World Olympic track and field events.

Dick Gregory, a well-known comedian and civil rights activist, was a track star while attending Southern Illinois University. In his book *Nigger*, he describes what he thought and how he felt while running, and of his compelling drive to excel. Wilma Rudolph, famous black track woman, could not walk until she was eight years old, but "a gruelling training program, the constant effort to excel, led her to Olympic victories." (John Davis, "The Negro in American Sports," *The American Negro Reference Book*, Prentice Hall, 1966.)

Gregory, before entering college, was a track champion in high school, but in his last race before high school graduation he placed seventeenth in a track field of seventeen. At the time he was insecure about what he wanted, what opportunities were open to him and he also neglected to keep in training. It is not a special diet or a special (racial) physical build that makes great black athletes anymore than is the case for whites. It is a matter, rather, of what can be represented by the formula C-O-M (capability, opportunity and motivation) or C-O-D (competency, opportunity and desire). Given the chance to participate and receive training to develop competency or capability, a black athlete, if he has desire or motivation to suceed, can become outstanding — just as for the white athlete. In certain cases, it may be that the black athlete trains a little harder. He may have a greater intensity of desire or motivation to win in competition. He may be given impetus by the feeling that his success helps give the lie to white sterotypes holding blacks to be inferior. It may be that because there have been relatively fewer outlets for blacks to demonstrate excellence, that sports attracts a disproportionate share of the talented young black population.

Among black people in meetings and in conversations a commonly-heard phrase is, "Tell it like it is." (Sometimes shortened to "Tell it.") This phrase conveys the meaning that a speaker is telling the truth, and is being encouraged by the listener(s) to go "right on" revealing the truth. In cases of a speaker distorting facts, telling half-truths, relating myths rather than facts, or making false statements, "Tell it *like it* is!" means "stop it . . . tell the truth!"

Most of us are born with an ability for telling it or seeing it "like it really is" or as we understand it to be. However, as we grow older, we learn that we must temper that ability with good judgment, born of experience. This ability is important and must not be stifled, but should be developed in order to be used when absolutely needed as in the case of racial distortions. If we have learned to think of others in terms of stereotypes, which are either distortions of reality or myths, we are hindered in developing the ability to "tell it like it is." Our stereotypes, serving as blinders, prevent us from recognizing and dealing with problems on a common human basis. Getting rid of our inaccurate, derogatory stereotypes does not mean we should go to an opposite extreme and over-idealize a group. To "tell it like it is" means that we recognize others as humans, even as we are human, with faults and frailities; with the need for understanding, encouragement, and help; with the right to equal opportunity to participate, develop and achieve — even as we claim this right for ourselves. In short, we truly need to mature, to grow up. In this regard we may do well to ponder the words of Saint Paul:

> When I was a child, I spake as a child, I understood as a child, I thought as a child: but when I became a man, I put away childish things.
> For now we see through a glass, darkly, but then face to face: now I know in part; but then shall I know even also I am Known.

# SIX

# RACE, COLOR, MARRIAGE

*Then it dawned upon me with a certain suddenness that I was different from the others or like, mayhap, in heart and life and longing, but shut out from their world by a vast veil* — W.E.B. Dubois, *The Souls of Black Folks.*

The founding fathers of our nation had a healthy respect for the foibles, and the darker side, of human nature. In the Federalist Paper Number 10 Madison remarked: "So strong is this propensity of mankind to fall into mutual animosities that where no substantial occasion presents itself the most frivolous and fanciful distinctions have been sufficient to kindle their unfriendly passions and excite their most violent conflicts." The truth of this observation has been more than amply demonstrated since it was written. Witness today the bloody conflict in Ireland between members of a racially homogeneous, but religiously divided people. In the United States (though not alone here) we continue to make distinctions on the basis of color. Such distinctions are a detriment to minority groups and militate against all groups living harmoniously with one another. And, it seems that most people believe that color is somehow a determinant of race or vice-versa.

We see someone or a group of people of color (going so far as to perceive them as all looking alike) and make assumptions as to the individual's or group's behavior patterns, capabilities and intelligence. We discriminate and segregate on the basis of color. We categorize people and cut ourselves off from entering into one-to-one, unique relationships with people. We define them, on the basis of color, as being different from and inferior to ourselves without having firsthand knowledge that this is so.

On the other hand, light-skinned people (people who are of, or who think they are of the white race) consider it esthetic and a mark of status to obtain a deep tan color of the skin by sun bathing or by means of ultra-violet lamps. No one would contend that because someone gets a deep tan he becomes inferior as a person! The point is there is no intrinsic relationship between skin color and behavioral qualities. It may also be noted there that blacks, black-skinned individuals, also "tan." That is, no matter how dark the skin, it can become darker by exposure to ultra-violet rays.

## Genetic Mixtures

Amram Scheinfeld in his *The Human Heredity Handbook* remarked: "If at a given time any human group was or is 'superior' in any respect, one could as easily ascribe this to their having been not pure but mixed, as in the case of Americans, one of the least racially 'pure' and most genetically mixed nationalities the world has seen." This genetic mixture has not been confined to those coming to this country from various parts of Europe. There has been considerable black-white (and Indian) intermixture since colonial times.

It has been estimated that at least 1 out of every 5 American Caucasians has Negro ancestry. Thousands of people yearly from black families adopt the white side of their heritage and cross over into the "white" race. These individuals do so to escape the pangs of discrimination suffered as a consequence of being identified as black; and to better their social and economic opportunities. Members of almost any black family in the United States can tell you of a relative — close or not too distant — who has cut his ties to family and friends and melted into the white scene.

On the other hand, the overwhelming majority of blacks have white ancestry. It, therefore, is possible for two dark-skinned blacks to have light complexioned children if they both carry genes for light skin color. The color of skin results from the amount and distribution, genetically determined, of a substance called melanin below the epidermis which shields out harmful sunrays; and, exposure to the sun results in the production of larger amounts of this pigment giving rise to suntan. Genes for facial and other features are carried independently of the genes controlling melanin deposits. Thus a very dark-skinned person can have "European" features and even blue eyes. It is surprising, but few people seem to be aware of the how or the why of skin coloration; and of why black Americans exhibit such a diversity of coloration and features.

114

## Intermarriage

Many people are curious about marriages between blacks and whites and ask such questions as: Do you think marriage between blacks and whites is moral? Should interracial marriages be advocated? Is it fair to children to be raised by interracial parents? If you marry a black person is it better to live in a white neighborhood or a black neighborhood? What kinds of problems do interracial couples have socially and between themselves?

Let us again point out that segregation in this country has no status in law. Marriage is a legal matter. Adults are free to enter into marriage under law. They are also entitled, legally, to live where they choose within their financial means. It is true that many states, mostly in the South, had laws which forbade interracial marriages until relatively recently; but the Supreme Court has now held such laws to be a denial of human rights and therefore unconstitutional.

Traditionally, in all societies, the primary purpose of marriage has been considered to be the propagation, rearing and protection of children. This has been considered the best means of insuring the continuity of the human race, its cultures, institutions and morals. It may or may not be immoral to have children out-of-legal-wedlock (depending often upon the complex set of circumstances.) But there can be no doubt that it certainly is moral to have children within the bonds of matrimony. Most people would agree that most of the time children are better off being reared by a mother and father in the home rather than being reared by a single parent with the child having no knowledge of his other parent. During the past 300 odd years, most of the black-white mixing that has taken place originated through relationships outside marriage — through concubinage, secret or open liaisons and rape — occurring primarily in the South. Both the fiery and brilliant abolitionist, Frederick Douglass, and the famous black educator, Booker T. Washington, were the sons of white fathers and slave mothers.

With the demise of legal prohibitions against interracial marriages, and the expansion of areas of association of blacks and whites (in employment, schools, the arts, etc.) it can be expected that interracial marriages will increase. As people begin to associate, get to know each other, find they have things in common, "fall in love," and perforce regard each other as persons with equal rights, privileges and duties, they will marry. Generally speaking, children of interracial marriages are and will be better off than those interracial children born out-of-legal-wedlock. They will enjoy the emotional and financial support provided by a mother and a father. They will enjoy the rights of inheritance, the benefits of insurance, social security, pensions, property, etc.

Some people, both black and white, who oppose interracial marriage, rationalize that children of such marriages will suffer from problems of identity; that their mixed color heritage will result in psychic turmoil and damage because of the negative attitudes of our "society" as it is now constituted. One answer to those who argue in this manner is: Since you see this as a problem for such children you should make sure that you yourself act decently and supportively toward such children and counsel others to do likewise; so that you and others you may influence do not contribute to damaging the emotional and mental health of these children.

## Children

Crocodile tears need not be shed for the plight of children of interracial parents. They may indeed receive emotional strength and a rich cultural heritage from their parents and families. In the past, and even now, light-skinned black children born of light-skinned black parents have suffered anguish and confusion because of the problem of color identification in a racist society. Some of them want to "be" and act white but must move almost exclusively within the confines of the black community. Others want to be black but are constantly rejected. The emergence in recent years of the concept of black pride, of the feeling of freedom to identify with one's blackness, has helped alleviate this problem. Children of interracial parents do and will have a problem of identifying with their blackness until such time as the color dichotomy as a basis for judgement is overcome.

On the whole, it is doubtful that the anguish and despair of those of mixed racial parentage compares with the anguish and despair inflicted upon their brothers of darker hue. Big Bill Broonzy, a black guitar playing blues singer from Mississippi used to sing a song with the words, "If you're white, you're all right; if you're brown, stick around'; if you're black, stand back." A black factory worker, in 1946 a recent migrant from the South, expressed himself this way: "Man, we is the asshole of de world." Twenty years later a wisp of a young, dark black girl from Mississippi said, "I didn't feel I was anybody until I heard Martin Luther King speak. He made me feel I could be somebody." A couple of years later, this young lady was working toward a degree at an interracial college in the North. Some black people in the past have, at times, in their anguish and despair over snubs, rebuffs and denials of opportunities bewailed their blackness and wished they had only been born white.

While objections to interracial marriages are generally thought of as coming from whites, there also are many blacks who voice disapproval. It seems that in the minds of some, one's blackness is paramount; and cohabiting, legally, with whites is somehow a betrayal of the cause of black liberation. Yet, so-called "black militant" intellectuals who voice such views often have friends and associates who are interracially married. In some inner-city ghetto areas, among the less educated, there is resentment against interracial dating and marriages. And in recent years there have been instances of violence against white male husbands and partners by black hoodlums. This is regrettable. It is a product of the generally violent atmosphere of the inner-city ghettos where there is a reservoir of hatred against whites, many of whom have exploited the black community, including the women. In years gone by, black-white couples were for the most part compelled to live in an all black area. Now there are some integrated small areas in the cities where they can live; or they can live in many of the suburbs. It is safer to live in such areas.

Racism, whether black or white, is ugly. The difference between them lies in the fact that white racism has been institutionalized; it has pervaded every area of life; it has denied black people their opportunities and rights; it has perpetuated countless horrors both psychological and physical with social and legal sanction; and has curtailed the freedom of whites of goodwill. Institutionalized hatred, hostility, and oppression has bred and always will breed hatred, hostility, and irrationality among the people toward whom

117

it is directed. As long as white racism persists so long will there be black racist backlashes and potentials for violence. Over a quarter of a century ago the great black writer and novelist, Richard Wright, remarked that white America had reduced the level of experience of the black in the ghetto to a crude and brutal level of experience with the potential for generating racial hate and violence; and this kind of situation persists today.

There are today, a number of black children growing up in homes, not of interracial parents, but of white parents and white brothers and sisters. These are children who have been adopted by white parents. As mentioned in an earlier chapter, adoption agencies for years provided the service of securing adoptive homes for white children born out-of-wedlock and blacks had little access to these agencies. Now the situation has changed. As the *New York Times* of January 20, 1973 put it:

> The adoption agencies, which were once able to provide a steady stream of white infants at fees ranging from $500 to $2000, have found that their sources have virtually dried up. A result: Waiting lists of from three to five years for a baby.
> The agencies have shifted their emphasis to children who used to be classified as "hard to place": They are either black or of mixed race, over the age of 2, or physically handicapped."

Black children adopted into white families can be considered fortunate as they will receive much love, attention, and security. They will know that they are black and loved for, or despite it. They need not have an identiy crisis of damaging proportions, but can feel secure in asserting themselves as human beings who do not have to feel guilt over being black. The white families who adopt black children and these children are hopefully bringing us closer to the ending of a racist society.

## Genocide

The ultimate development of racism is genocide — the attempt at extermination of a whole people considered to share certain traits

118

by racists who wield economic and political power. The German government headed by Adolf Hitler murdered 6 million Jews (who are not racially, in the genetic, and even the cultural sense, homogenous) and Slavs (Poles and inhabitants of the Balkan countries) who were deemed inferior by the killers who believed they were a "master race." This despite the fact that Jews and Slavs were represented in all areas of endeavor and held positions of prestige and renown.

This lesson of history has not been lost on blacks in this country. It is why some black intellectuals continue to speak of "tokenism." They feel that though economic progress has been made by numbers of blacks, and that while some blacks now occupy fairly prestigious positions in our society, the danger of genocide directed against blacks will continue to exist until American culture and institutions are entirely rid of racist attitudes of white superiority and of overt and covert discrimination. They see danger in any development that might be utilized by the present social and political structure to control or channel the behavior of blacks in a manner deemed desirable by the white prejudiced majority.

An example of this is the reaction of some black leaders to the decision in 1973 by the United States Supreme Court legalizing abortions. Some have denounced this decision on the basis of what they seem to consider to be genocide at the source, so to speak, and have called for its overturn. In the present economic structure of our nation, black population growth comes largely from blacks who are poor, among whom there are a large number of out-of-wedlock births, and who are involved with welfare agencies. It is feared by some that the power of the state will be used to coerce black women into terminating pregnancies in order to save money spent on public aid and in social services; and to control the growth of black population upon which, in large measure, black political power rests. The proponents of this view have adopted a position like that of the Roman Catholic Church that life begins at conception, and that it is morally wrong to deliberately abort a pregnancy at any stage.

Racism on the basis of color is not peculiar to the United States; which no more justifies its existence here than persecution of Protestants in some countries would justify their persecution here. Educators have no greater responsibility than to ensure that

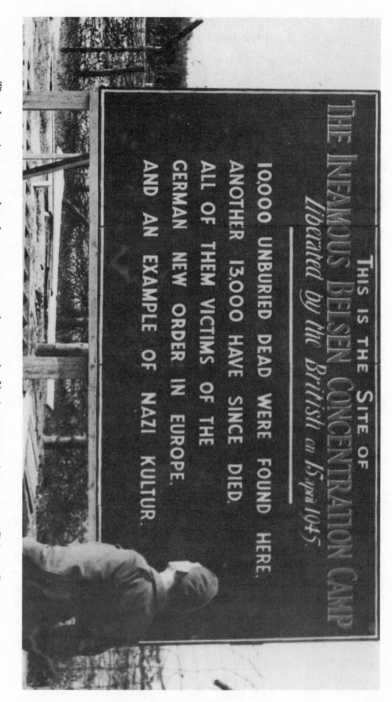

*The above sign, erected at the entrance to what was the Nazi concentration camp at Belsen, Germany, briefly presents statistics of the camp. A similar sign in German stands nearby. (Wide World Photo)*

*American Editors take notes as they view victims of the Buchenwald Concentration Camp in Germany in April 1945.* (Wide World Photo).

students learn the full meaning of the principles upon which our country was founded: all men are created equal and the purpose of government is the happiness and the welfare of the people. Educators can aid students to learn of the essential similarities of all men, the reasons for physical differences, the contributions of blacks and others to the building of our country, and the need and rightness of ridding ourselves of irrational hate. The problems of survival on this ever-shrinking planet demand the cooperative, liberated, intellectual, and emotional forces of each of us.

In November 1963, The General Assembly of the United Nations adopted a Universal Declaration of Human Rights, reminiscent of our Declaration of Independence, proclaiming that "all human beings are born free and equal in dignity and rights and that everyone is entitled to all those rights and freedoms, without distinction of any kind, in particular of race, color, or national origin . . . " To the extent we put these ideals into practice, to the extent that we realize them, to that extent do we realize our own humanity. To the extent that we fail to put into practice these universal ideals, to that extent do we fall short of being whole persons.

SEVEN

# INTEGRATION

*It seems by now almost generally accepted that the drive for desegregation in all its phases . . . must not slacken; and that the final act of the opening drama must see at long last the elimination of segregation and discrimination on racial, ethnic and religious grounds in our society.* Discrimination USA by Jacob K. Javits, United States Senator.

Why can't we have segregation? It's less trouble that way. Shouldn't Negroes work to improve their own class — rather than saying integration is the only solution to their problems? Why are Negroes in such a hurry to get complete integration — it was only a couple of hundred years ago that they were over in Africa . . . and we brought them from that dark and infested continent. Do you think the averge black wants to be integrated with white people? Do blacks prefer living in an integrated neighborhood or would they prefer living amongst their own — i.e. like the Polish in Humboldt Park, the Irish in "Back of the Yards" area in Chicago, the Jews in Rogers Park, etc.? Are integrated schools or segregated schools better? Why? What do you think is the most important step toward acceptance of an equal multi-racial society? What should Caucasians do? What should blacks do?

"Integration" means living together. It means free association with each other, learning together and sharing experiences. It cannot be said that integration, or even movement toward integration, does or would create violence. The opposite is true. The violence that has and continues to occur around the issue of integration is a result of resistance to integration. Often black families are harassed, threatened, burned, and pillaged on moving into a white neighborhood; and black students are often discriminated against, harassed and tormented on entering predominantly white schools. Put another way, violence results from efforts to maintain or re-establish segregation.

123

# THE LIFESTYLE OF BLACK PEOPLE

## Neighborhood Violence

Added to this kind of violence is the great amount of violence which occurs within the ghettos — robberies, burglaries, beatings, rapes, killings. And wherever the ghetto encroaches the rates of these crimes go up. Black families who find decent homes in areas adjacent to the expanding ghetto soon see their hopes for living in a safe, relatively quiet, peaceful neighborhood shattered. The undesirable, violent, raucous behavior so prevalent in the ghetto and which they sought to escape, in the move to newer neighborhoods, follows them. The "nice" neighborhood into which they moved swiftly changes.

Whites begin to move out to the suburbs. Blacks of the poorer classes, always hard-pressed to find housing in a housing shortage market, many of them dispossessed of living space by urban renewal programs, now move in large numbers where they can — into the areas where one or a few black families have moved and which the whites begin to flee. The density of population increases, rents increase while services — street cleaning, garbage removal, building maintenance, and most importantly, school facilities — do not. The area begins to take on a bleak, run-down appearance. Stores close and move either because of the declining economic level or because of intimidation by gangs who, as the complexion and population density of the neighborhood change, feel free to roam. Drug addicts and pushers likewise appear in increasing numbers, with addicts engaging in theft, robbery and prostitution to support their habits.

This sequence of events has occurred so many times, that many black people are convinced that powerful elements of the white power structure deliberately connive to create these conditions; that this is done for the purpose of preparing for the wholesale repression — even genocide — of black people. In the vernacular of some ghetto residents, "If it ain't true, it sure *do* look that way." It is not the process of achieving integration that is responsible for generating violence in ghetto areas and those areas undergoing racial transistion, but the processes of resistance and resegregation.

Resistance to integration is a stark and massive fact. There can be no doubt that this resistance is a primary source of conflict in our society and a source of misery for many people. One of the terrible things about our present situation of resistance to

124

integration is that people of good will — both black and white — become victims of criminal depredations and violence in changing neighborhoods and schools. For instance, around the first of September, 1971 two thirteen-year-olds, a white boy and a white girl, were shot to death by young black men in a racially changing area. The father of the dead girl wrote the following letter:

Dear Friends and Neighbors:

Duffie Clark is black. I am white. A while back I heard a commotion going on; so I walked down the street. I saw this young black man and his dog. I asked what was wrong. He said some boys were throwing things at him and his dog. I got my dog and walked him home, telling him how sorry I was that these people were being so cruel to him.

I also tried to make him understand that we are not all so mean and hateful as this. We shook hands after he introduced two other black men to me as his brothers. He was asked by me to please come to my home anytime he had any kind of problem and I would attempt to help him anytime of the day or night. The next time I heard of Duffie Clark was when I was told he had killed my girl. My daughter upon being informed that there were black people coming to St. John's [school] this year, said, "Daddy, I'll be their friend." Yet she was shot down in cold blood. She was as innocent as many of you who read this.

I am pleading with those of you who are my neighbors and know what happened to the weapon that struck my girl down to come forward and help save some other black or white human from being senselessly destroyed. In this way we can come closer to loving and understanding one another.

Also by helping recover the weapon used, we can help this man, Duffie Clark, should he be innocent. For so help me God, we have got to reach out our hands in love and understanding or we have nothing. May God bless and please forgive us all for our intolerance.

Sam Navarro

Helene's Dad

If integration means free association, learning together and sharing experiences, why, one wonders, would anyone oppose it? Why would some people rather resort to violence to prevent the coming together of people and perpetuate racial hostility by example and by indoctrinating their children than to seek to live together and meet common problems together? The reader may try an experiment and ask of himself or of any of his acquaintances who are opposed to integration these questions and see if he can get a rational answer.

## Busing, and the Neighborhood School

Today, in the United States of America, segregation has no sanction in law; integration does have sanction in law. Although this is true, many people are confused about the legal status of integration — largely because of statements made by influential people in local, state and federal governments including the President of the United States. President Nixon has stated on the one hand that he is opposed to busing pupils to achieve educational integration; and, on the other, he does not feel government should try to enforce residential integration in suburban communities.

However, in April 1971, the United States Supreme Court held that busing is perfectly proper as a means of achieving racial integration in public schools — upholding decisions by Federal Judges who had ordered busing to carry out the intent of the 1954 Supreme Court decision which held that separate educational facilities for Negroes and whites are inherently unequal. The Supreme Court also let stand a decision by a Federal Judge in Chicago ordering the Chicago Housing Authority to build public housing in predominantly white neighborhoods and to place three black families in such neighborhoods for every one black family placed in the ghetto.

The Mayor of this great and important city prior to his reelection in April 1971, stated he would defy the court order. After his reelection, under the threat of cut-off of federal funds to the city, the mayor announced compliance to the ruling; but the local government has been moving reluctantly and has been threatened again with the withholding of federal funds. In this controversy, the mayor has made an important and constructive suggestion to the effect that residential integration should be sought not merely on a city-wide basis (because people will continue to move to the suburbs) but on a metropolitan basis.

The U.S. Department of Education found in 1966 that when measured by the "yardstick" of the 1954 Supreme Court decision,

> . . . American public education remains largely unequal in most regions of the country, including all those where Negroes form any significant proportion of the population.

The study, *Equality of Educational Opportunity*, was concerned with the effects of desegregated schools on pupil achievement. Results of the study show that in general, black pupils benefited greatly in desegregated schools while the achievement level of white pupils did not decline. The study also found that white students who at early ages attended integrated schools valued their association with black students; and that the smallest percentage of white students who "would choose all white classes or all white friends are those who first attended classes with non-whites in the early grades." The study furthermore found that black pupils in integrated schools where most of the pupils were white had a greater sense of control and feeling that they determined their own destiny. Would we not say, on the basis of these findings, that integrated schools are better than segregated schools?

In 1968, Meyer Weinberg who edits a magazine, *Integrated Education* published a book *Desegregation Research: An Appraisal* which reported the findings of numerous studies on the effects of desegregated education in elementary and secondary schools. His conclusions on the basis of the research done were essentially the same as those of the Commission on Education. Weinberg also points out that a desegregated or integrated school should be distinguished from a transitional school:

> . . . The latter type is an all-white school in the process of becoming a predominantly Negro school; whereas a desegregated school is characterized by a stable inter-racial student body. Obviously, the setting in a transitional school is highly unfavorable to constructive and productive student relations. Confusion of the two types is not uncommon.

This is the type of school we get as the ghetto expands at the fringe areas occupied by whites who begin to flee and resegregate the school. Weinberg also points out that in the integrated school, the self-esteem of black children rise and there is increased self-acceptance as a black person.

Black parents, like white parents, want the best possible education for their children; and many black youths want to get a good education. Black parents are aware that their children are being cheated of the best possible public school education in the over-crowded, gang-infested ghetto schools. These are schools to which many children walk in fear — fear of shakedowns from gangs and pressures from gang members to join the gangs. And, many blacks are aware that in all likelihood their children will get a better education in a school outside the ghetto.

But, how is the child to get outside the confines of the ghetto to get his education? Safely and in a reasonable time? By bus, of course.

A great furor has been created over the busing of students, with many people contending it is wrong not to let a child attend his "neighborhood" school. The bus and the "neighborhood school" have become symbols of opposition to integration. Yet, not too many years ago civil rights advocates in the North were asking that black children be allowed to attend the schools nearest their homes. At that time segregation was maintained by sending black children to schools within the confines of the ghetto, even though they might live closer to a school not attended by all black children. Today, with the expanded ghetto areas which have engulfed many previously all-white schools, segregation is more easily maintained by having children attend schools nearest home which are most likely to be in the ghetto confines.

Busing and the neighborhood school are really not the issues. The white people who overturn, burn, and bomb buses and who picket children getting on and off the buses are not defending their children from the "rigors" of riding a bus to school or the sanctity of the school building in their locality. Not at all. Through their actions they are saying that they do not want their children to attend school with black children; that blacks are inferior and should be kept in separate schools.

School children and youth have long been bused in this country — to public and private nursery schools, kindergartens, special schools for the handicapped, and high schools. And, busing has been used to maintain segregation in the public schools. For instance, in a 1969 suit brought by the U.S. District Attorney's Office against the Cook County Illinois school district of South Holland, it was established that white high school students were bused across town to attend a school of all white students, passing a high school reserved for blacks along the way. Nevertheless, the school district appealed the District Court order to integrate the schools, and lost the appeal. In 1971, a federal judge in Detroit determined that busing had been used to maintain segregation in the public schools of that city. In 1972, Denver integrated its schools using busing as one means. It now seems that the judiciary is determined, that segregation sanctioned by public officials shall cease. As a result, there are likely to be more suits involving big cities in the near future.

## The Black Experience

The "average" black person in this country does not go around thinking how nice it would be to be integrated with white people. Like the "average" white person, he does go around thinking it would be nice to have a good job, live in a good neighborhood, have a lot of money, give the kids a good education, etc. As James Baldwin remarked in his book *The Fire Next Time:*

There appears to be a vast amount of confusion on this point, but I do not know many Negroes who are eager to be "accepted" by white people, still less to be loved by them; they, the blacks, simply don't want to be beaten over the head by the whites every instant of our brief passage on this planet. White people in this country will have quite enough to do in learning how to accept and love themselves and each other, and when they have achieved this — which will not be tomorrow and may very well be never — the Negro problem will no longer exist, for it will not longer be needed.

The experience of blacks in this country has been compared to the experience of foreign immigrant groups who have also been victims of prejudice and discrimination; who also had high incidences of social problems — crime, delinquency, drunkeness, illegitimate births, etc. associated with large scale poverty and the difficulties of adjusting to big city life. Many descendants of immigrants express the view that "We had it hard too; but we worked, sacrificed, raised ourselves up. People gotta raise themselves by their own bootstraps." The implication here — a false one — is that blacks have not or do not try to raise themselves, etc.

The migration of blacks from the rural, often primitive areas of the South in large numbers, many of them illiterate or barely literate (but others of them who are quite literate and informal) to the large American cities may be compared to the migrations of the millions of poor from the various European countries. These migrations, in search of jobs and a greater amount of freedom (on the part of both the European immigrants and the native American blacks) are similar in terms of problems of adjustment by the poor and uneducated to urban life. There are the same problems of finding housing, finding a job, getting enough money to pay the rent and buy the food, getting an education, keeping the children from bad associations, etc. As the *Kerner Report* points out ". . . nostalgia makes it easy to exaggerate the ease of escape of the white immigrants from the ghettos." The report goes on to state:

> . . . among many of the Southern and Eastern Europeans who came to America in the last great wave of immigration, whose who came already urbanized were the first to escape from poverty. The others who came to America from rural backgrounds . . . are only now, after three generations, in the final stages of escaping from poverty. Until the last 10 years or so, most of these were employed in blue-colar jobs, and only a small proportion of their children were able or willing to attend college. In other words, only the third, and in many cases the fourth generation has been able to achieve the kind of middle-class income and status that allows it to send its children to college.

Anyone who is really familiar with the life of black people in the cities has seen and sees the striving for educational and economic betterment in black families; and knows of many second generation blacks who now hold professional, managerial, clerical, and sales positions. Many there are today from poor homes (some broken, some not) who through hard work and perseverance have attained middle-class status; or are continuing to strive for advancement.

It is one of those oddities of human behavior, if one stops to think, that people who express wonder as to why blacks do not lift themselves up by their own bootstraps are people who in one way or another deny blacks the rights and privileges of our society. And, while European immigrants to our country often felt the sting of discrimination, there has been one fundamental difference in their experience — *they were not segregated and discriminated against by law.*

## The Effect of Law

The black man has been by law, in his own country, held not to be entitled to full rights of citizenship. By law he has been deliberately segregated on the basis of the color of his skin. Legal segregation buttressed and encouraged attitudes and beliefs that black people were not quite wholly human beings. Segregationist laws and the expressions of hate they encouraged made the black man fair game for any and every kind of discrimination and brutality. The European immigrants readily added prejudice against blacks to their old country prejudices against other peoples with which they arrived.

The importance of the law, of the legal status of people with skin pigmentation and features identified as Negroid or black, cannot possibly be overestimated. It is surprising how many people do not realize the extent to which their own actions are conditioned, limited, and determined by the laws of the country. Many people who believe that blacks are naturally inferior are really merely expressing what they have been encouraged to believe by the sanctioned segregation and discrimination they have seen. Laws of the land can either further or hinder our expressions of good will toward others.

In Tulsa, Oklahoma, a group of about 100 mothers in 1971 began voluntarily to send their children by bus to black schools in the city. They did so on the basis that their children's education

# THE LIFESTYLE OF BLACK PEOPLE

*Black ladies in back of bus pointing to segregation sign which became void April 26, 1956 following a ruling by the U.S. Supreme Court. (UPI Photo).*

132

*Black soldier looking at segregation signs in Georgia in 1956.* (UPI Photo)

should include getting to know blacks with whom they will have to live in their country. While the actions of these mothers was voluntary, it could occur because the law of the land permits and encourages integration. In an atmosphere of legal repression, where the law or the courts hold segregation to be proper and desirable, parents would not take such action because they would be without legal support.

Segregationists are well aware of the importance of law and the enforcement of laws in conditioning peoples' outlook and attitudes toward others. That is why they have fought so hard against civil rights legislation and enforcement of this legislation. Although it was in 1954 that the Supreme Court declared school segregation unconstitutional, people are still fighting to keep black students separated (segregated) with the aid and encouragement of law. Congressmen representing the school segregationist viewpoint have been and are still trying to forbid the government from spending any money to bus pupils, or requiring the states to spend money for busing, and to require that court-ordered integration go through lengthy appeals in the hope of stalling integration. If children get together, learn the same things together and about each other, are taught that we are all the same and equal human beings, then we, all of us, would be saved from the problems of worrying about who or who is not "equal" on the basis of such irrevelant characteristics as skin color. It is sad to remark that the parents of our children, who themselves were supposed to have been taught better, continue to teach their children the ways of hate and discrimination rather than the ways of love and acceptance.

## Open Housing

Several days after the assassination of Martin King Luther, Jr. in April 1968, Congress passed and President Lyndon Johnson signed into law the National Fair Housing Act forbidding discrimination on the basis of color or race in the rental or sale of housing anywhere in the United States. The passage of this law has opened the way for black families, particularly those in the middle and upper income levels, to move into metropolitan suburban areas from which they were formerly excluded by practices of real estate agencies and attitudes of white homeowners. During the past five years, a beginning of a movement of black families to the formerly all-white suburbs has begun.

As yet this movement has been small relative to the numbers of black families who are able financially to qualify for such housing. One reason for this has been fear on the part of many blacks of rejection, harassment or violence by whites in the suburban areas. This fear has been largely proved unfounded. White suburbs have become safer for blacks to move into than white areas within the city. Violence against blacks moving into white areas within the city persists. Paul A. Epstein, executive director of the Home Investment Fund, operating in the Chicago metropolitan area has remarked:

> Of all the families Home Improvement has helped, not one has moved [away] because of harassment. In fact, many have become quite active in their communities, serving on planning boards and human relations groups. If there is any harassment, certainly it doesn't measure up to the kind black families experience when they move into formerly all-white neighborhoods in the city. (*Chicago Tribune*, April 19, 1973)

Home Investment Fund is a non-profit corporation organized in 1968 by the Chicago Conference on Religion and Race to help minority families move into the white suburbs; and it has helped get housing for some 400 families during the past five years. Home Investment Fund could come into being and be of as much help as it has in achieving integration because of the National Fair Housing law giving sanction to those acting from good-will. It is through activities of such groups (and the individuals comprising them) as HIF, actively promoting good will and understanding, offering practical help to people now able legally to take advantage of long denied opportunities, that acceptance of a multi-racial society may be brought about.

At another, and more basic level, there can be little doubt that our schools are of primary importance in preparing our young people for integrated living. The schools themselves have been primary targets for the process of desegregation, which in and of

Black family shown in the back yard of their suburban home.

(Chicago Sun-Times Photo)

itself does not insure the achievement of integration. Desegregation of schools, particularly in large urban areas, generates a number of problems between the students themselves, between students and teachers, and between the school and the community. And while legally our society has committed itself to desegregation, psychologically there remains massive resistance to it. This is unfortunate, creating tensions and violent conflict in the process of desegregation which would be considerably lessened if there were massive psychological committment to desegregation.

Too often, particularly in the large urban areas, school desegregation has been merely a phase on the way to resegregation instead of on the way to integration — white families fleeing their residences as black enrollments increased in the schools. Once this process is set in motion, it seems almost impossible to stop. It is one reason why the courts have had to resort to the ordering of busing of pupils. It has been the only way to meet the requirement of desegregated education.

At this juncture it appears that the process of desegregation will, however smoothly or haltingly, continue. And for those who teach, counsel, or administrate in our nation's schools — whether they are presently segregated black schools, lily-white schools, or desegregated schools — it is very important they be aware of racial problems that are encountered or are likely to be encountered as desegregation proceeds; as well as the background and situational reasons for the problems. School personnel are interested and concerned, and, like the students and others in the general populace, have many questions on their minds. It is to the questions and problems expressed by those entrusted to the education of our children that the next section is devoted.

# PART II

# BLACK AND WHITE

# PERSPECTIVES ON

# EDUCATION AND LEARNING

# EIGHT

# BLACK PARENTS AND THE SCHOOL

*A soft answer turneth away wrath: but grievous words stir up anger.* Proverbs, St. James Version of the Holy Bible.

Do black parents want their children disciplined according to white standards of classroom behavior? Do black parents encourage their children to mistreat white teachers in school? Do black parents of below average income share common feelings as a group . . . that the answers to many of their problems is education or more aid from government agencies? Do black parents really want school integration for their children? How do they feel about busing? Why don't black parents take more interest in their children's schooling? Why don't they come to the school to discuss with the teacher problems their child is having? When a black parent comes to school angry because of punishment a white teacher has administered to his (her) child, how do you handle the situation? Why do some black parents advocate community control, by blacks, of schools and try to get rid of white principals and teachers?

These are questions which have often been asked by white teachers. Quite recently, many of these questions were raised in a race relations workshop of teachers in a Northern school district, who face impending desegregation of their schools. Most of these teachers seemed to want to gain real understanding of the problems of integration. They expressed the desire to make integrated education work, to provide good education for both blacks and whites, to avoid conflict based on prejudice and hostility. Their backgrounds ranged from middle to lower class; of mixed Scotch, Irish, English, German, Scandanavian, French, Italian, and Slavic descent; of largely Protestant and Catholic religious heritage. They had taught school from one to many years — some in schools with a few blacks, some in schools with no blacks, some in ghetto schools, and some in schools that were one-third black, the rest white. Some had had little or no association with black people in their entire lives.

## Discipline

All of us, black, white, red, yellow and brown are faced with the problem of "discipline"—particularly in regard to the rearing and education of our children. And, in a personal sense, all of us are faced throughout our lives with disciplining ourselves in various areas of our lives — our occupations, financial responsibilities, family responsibilities, eating and drinking habits, and so on. In a general way all of us feel that it is up to the family and the school to impart discipline in order that the growing person will be able to fulfill his moral and social obligations as he reaches maturity. We have been far from perfect in this matter, as witness, for example, the appalling degree of "white collar" crime — embezzlements, stock and loan frauds, political "dirty tricks" and worse. Part of the teacher's task is learning professional discipline — the application of knowledge and skills in a manner that respects the integrity and fosters the growth of pupils.

It is safe to say that most black parents do not conceive of the schoolroom as being a place where there is to be one standard of behavior for white children and another for black. They believe, in general, that "correct" behavior in the classroom should be a human standard that everyone understands; and they caution their children that if they do not behave and get their lessons they will not pass. Many black parents feel, however, that there does exist among teachers a "double standard" of discipline. Many are afraid that their children will be made to "toe the line" while the more privileged white child will be able to do whatever he or she likes and get away with it. There does exist resentment among black parents as to the manner in which their children have been treated in regard to discipline and also grading. Here are some examples of the kinds of experiences which have led to suspicion and resentment on the part of black parents:

A black parent visiting a high school saw a white, male teacher slap a black girl. When she inquired as to what happened she was told that the girl called the teacher a name. A white teacher reported an incident at one school where a black girl was suspended for dancing on potato chips. Some high school students relate an incident where a white student who was harassing a white teacher stated to the teacher and class at large that his parents paid her (the teacher's) salary and that he didn't have to do anything he didn't want. A black student yelled "I second that!" and was suspended for a week, while the white student got off with only a verbal reprimand. A white substitute teacher states she was passing by an open classroom door and saw a white male teacher bend a teen-age black girl over his desk and whack her repeatedly on the rear-end with his hand. A black male high school student stated that his counselor (white) had him suspended for almost a month, because some black students staged a school "walk out." He had not engaged in the activity and his teacher admitted that he had stayed in class; however in the excitement, she had forgotten to indicate that he was present on the daily class roster. His suspension, however, was not lifted.

A black male adult relates that when he attended a predominantly white school many years ago, his math teacher told him if he would be quiet and not ask any questions in class he would get a "C" for the course. He got the "C" but did not learn the math (until much later with the aid of "brush-up" night courses in math). A black high school student tells of an incident where a teacher repeatedly demanded that he bring his mother to the school to discuss his attendance record. His mother was not formally educated (having gone only to the third grade in elementary school), worked to support the family, and was fearful of going to the school and being embarrassed in front of her son. She was finally convinced by her son to take off from work and visit the teacher. The teacher, however, chose that time to refuse to see his mother on the grounds that she should have come earlier. Both mother and son suffered hurt, shame, anger and humiliation. A social worker tells of an incident in a grade school he visited where the white, female assistant principal had a girl's bow tied around the head of a little black boy as punishment for some infraction.

For those interested in learning of more extreme and bizarre forms of "disciplinary" measures, both corporal and psychical, meted out to black children by whites, a reading of Jonathan Kozol's account of his experience in the Boston public school system a few years ago, entitled *Death at an Early Age*, is recommended.

Black parents do not resent discipline as such, but they do, just as white parents, object to their child being subjected to cruel and unusual punishment. And they object to discipline degenerating into either black or white discipline. Many black parents can conceive of honest discipline used to aid the growth of a student's potential.

Discipline is seen as a problem by teachers in all settings, but in ghetto or transitional schools, the problem may seem overwhelming. For the teacher, however, the development of children's potential and creativity should have top priority. Probably the most demanding challenge a teacher has is to develop discipline through fostering creativity. Some years ago, the American sociologist, W.I. Thomas, posited "four wishes" or desires as the springs of human behavior: the desire for recognition, desire for response, desire for security, and desire for new experience. Recognition by teachers of these basic needs and the attempt to relate to students in terms of them can be a fruitful and rewarding approach. Here is an example:

One white, female teacher in an all black ghetto school encourages her fourth graders to write creatively. She then helps them compile a class book with all the stories in them which everyone can read. She, as well as the students, enjoys this activity which certainly would seem to be rewarding for all. Here is one of the youngster's stories:

### If I Had a Magic Pencil

One day I went to school and I didn't have a pencil. So I was walking across the playground and I saw a shiny gold pencil and I picked it up and I went in school. When I got in the classroom my teacher said, "Douglas, do you have a pencil?" and I said 'yes'." When I wrote my story I went to sharpen my pencil. When I came back I looked at my paper and there was not a scratch on the paper. So I put a mark on the paper and I stood there and the mark disappeared. I pointed the pencil at a girl and she disappeared. I pointed the pencil at myself and I dis-

appeared and it got out of hand and everything started to disappear.
By Douglas Green.

There are black students who certainly present behavior and disciplinary problems; and in some schools, particularly in the heart of the big-city ghettos, they can loom large. But even here, most of the students are not constantly disruptive and incorrigible; they have their dreams and hopes of bettering themselves through education. Many are badly cheated by a school system which does not seem to have enough time or interest to devote to them.

Sometimes what a teacher might perceive as a discipline problem might really just be a style of behavior not intended to bring on disfavor — or to be taken as a deliberate show of hostility. On occasion, a black child's face may look hostile, but the right words can quickly bring a smile and an easing of tensions. Those black students who at first wore a "natural" were thought to be very militant and apt to be cracked-down on "quick and hard" at the first sign of intractability. Now most teachers regard the "natural" as simply another hair style.

Behavior and disciplinary problems, even severe ones, are by no means the monoply in our society of black students. Probably, as integration proceeds, we will be able to more and more see behavioral problems as common human ones, rather than associating the bad with black and the better and good with white. This matter had been stated very well by a young white girl attending a suburban high school. She was commenting on remarks made in a newspaper column about conditions in ghetto schools and the students' behavior. She says:

> I go to a public school in a suburb. In it we have poor, low-middle class (me) and high middle-class people. And the conditions you've mentioned in black schools aren't all that much different from mine, which is not integrated. One thing is the swearing. I've come to the conclusion that rich or poor, smart or slow, we all swear alike. We use the same words, maybe not with the same degree of frequency, but we use them. And it's not unusual for someone to swear in the classroom. Everyone just snickers and turns

to the teacher who usually pretends not to hear. That's the best thing to do, after all, they're just words. We also give substitutes trouble. Everyone feels a sense of freedom with the regular gone. We do everything against the rules just for kicks. Needless to say, no one ever learns anything from a substitute. Maybe black parents should encourage their kids more. Yeah, maybe they should, but they should be careful they don't copy the white parents. Among them there seems to be no 'happy medium.' Either the parents don't care and neither do the kids; or the parents care too much about the 'status' connected with a smart kid — which creates different problems. Too-anxious parents have kids who either become the most apathetic vulgar creeps away from home or just plain nervous wrecks.

What I'm trying to say is that it's not fair to blame the black kids for not caring, as if the problem were only theirs. It's just that no one wants to admit that we have the exact same problems, including old books and teachers, shifts because of over-crowding and full-time cops just itching to arrest somebody. These problems are universal, but most kids don't even recognize these as problems, and that's sad.

Many black parents fear that white teachers who discipline their children may be using discipline as a means to get "even" for the fact that they are in the school in the first place. Black parents, like most white parents, do not wish to have their children manhandled or disciplined unfairly. They want the same treatment for the same infraction as the white students receive, no more and no less. Hostility flowing from a white child is no more attractive than hostility flowing from a black child, and the teacher must be aware that the whole idea of discipline is meant to channel the students' energies in another, more creative path.

### Teacher and Parent

Black parents, like most other parents, do not encourage their children to either mistreat or harass any school teacher. However, some black parents do not like certain white persons who have touched their lives in a negative fashion, and they are not silent about their feelings on the matter while at home. Some black students may take this to mean that they do not have to take anything from any white teacher; in essence, a strike at the white system through the white teacher, is a blow in the favor of black freedom.

Students can sometimes influence their parents into believing that the teacher is against them (the students) solely because they are black. Sometimes, because the parents both work, or are absent from the home much of the time, a student may not even have to exert any negative influence against the teacher and in favor of himself. Such parents are virtually unreachable by the school administration anyway. While these students are not the majority they cannot be ignored. Somehow, they must be shown a new road which leads to self-discipline. But they first must understand why a new "road" is necessary. They must learn what it is they are doing that must be corrected, why the correction is necessary, and realize that they themselves can make things better for their own individual futures.

One way of helping the student into this awareness is to get a positive response from the parents. The quickest way to do this is to give the parents a report that speaks first of the strengths the student has; coupled with a plea for help from the parent in the area where it is felt the student has need. Most parents, black or white, will back up a teacher when they feel she or he is doing the best possible for their child.

## Welfare and Busing

Quite a few teachers who have never taught or lived in areas where black people live wonder if blacks are more interested in welfare than education for their children. Most black people on welfare view it as a temporary necessity. They wish for their children the attainment of a "good" education, one that leads to college or to a fine trade school. Their hope is that either of these avenues of education will enable their children to obtain positions or jobs making enough money to prevent them from ever "landing" on welfare. Most black people, especially the poor, view federal aid

*Mrs. Camilla Guthrie and Mrs. Mary Carr and their daughters, Patricia and Ethel Mai, were the first to arrive and take their place in line for registration on August 27, 1957 at a previously all-white school in Nashville, Tennessee. Nashville started its desegration program by integrating the first grades only.*
(AP Wirephoto)

in scholarships as good, and encourage their children to find out all they can about how to get one. They feel there is no shame in accepting such a scholarship because it is a temporary measure, which they help to pay for in taxes, and designed to aid a student intent on furthering his education.

Then there are some black parents who feel the whole educational system, as far as their children are concerned, is a farce. But, in spite of their beliefs, they still urge their children to at least get a high school diploma so as to get a worthwhile job when they graduate. The problems black people have had to face emphatically include exclusion from the main stream of American middle-class life. Most realize that getting a "good" education can be the difference between entering the busy "main stream" of American life-style and pridefully contributing or "slipping and sliding" toward the dead-end street of public welfare.

Here is one black parent's views on governmental aid:

> If you mean by 'aid from government agencies' community jobs, like meter maids or something, I'm for it. But only to help my kids get a better education than I did. But if you mean, 'do I want my kids to grow up and get on welfare,' then you need your head examined. Would anybody want that for their kids? If there is no other way, my kids have to eat, but if they get a good education, then they don't ever have to even think of welfare!

Most black parents of below average income feel that education is the key to success and they want to be able to hand that key to their children.

When black parents think of voluntarily sending their children to a white school in a white neighborhood, it is not for the sake of their children having a chance to simply sit next to a white child, or of being taught by a white teacher. It is because they believe that the potential for a better, more thorough education is greater in a white middle-class school. These parents believe that graduation from such a school will enhance their child's chances of acceptance in a prestige college or university. When a child is enrolled in an upper middle-class elementary or high school, there are many extra benefits he will most likely be exposed to; not the least of these being more individualized attention from the teacher in a smaller class.

Many black parents have to make their economic way in the white world. They realize that integration is a solution to most of the misunderstandings they find facing them in the few contacts they have with whites. They feel they know much more about white people than whites know about them. They believe the only way to reconcile fact and myth is to know each other equally well. Therefore, most black parents do want school integration as a start for their children. But they do not want to put their children in jeopardy in the process. As to how they feel about busing, there is a consensus of opinion that voluntary busing of black children to white schools is an individual matter and certainly all right, but as to "forced" busing here is what some black parents have to say:

> We aren't against busing, but we feel that two-way busing
> of white as well as black students would be much fairer
> than just busing black kids.

White opponents to busing to desegregate the schools suddenly find themselves shoulder to shoulder with blacks opposing the same thing, but for different reasons. Black parents feel the burden is always placed upon the minorities to accomplish what the majority is constantly fighting. Some of the black parents facing "forced" busing had this to say:

> Right now my child only has to walk two blocks to school
> and she's never late. But what if she misses the bus, and
> I've gone to work, who will look after her? Where will she
> go and how will I know where she is? If I have to bus my
> child, I will simply take her out of school!

> My child's friends all live here around the school, now
> when he goes to the new school across town, he won't have
> any friends he can grow up with, and have fun with,
> because the whites won't let them be friends.

> In my own neighborhood, I can go and visit the principal
> or my child's teacher anytime I want to; but when my

150

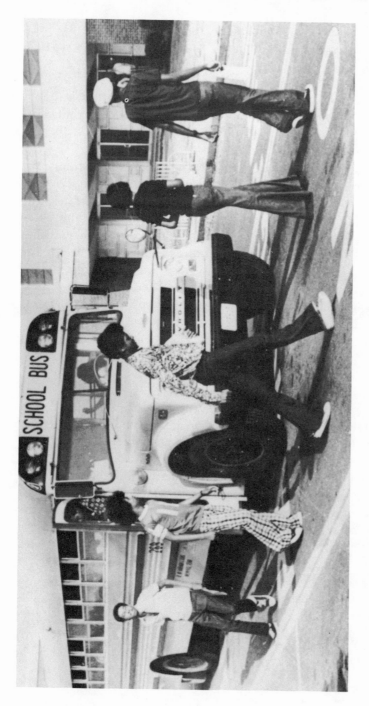

*One of 155 buses discharges passengers at a school on August 28, 1973 on the first day of widescale desegregation busing in Memphis, one of the South's largest school systems. Buses ran late, two were in minor accidents and some pupils were stranded after school, but officials rated the peaceful day a success. About 27,000 children rode, 13,000 fewer than forecast in a judge's busing order.*

(AP Wirephoto)

child's school is 30 miles away, how can I do that? And will I be safe if I go into the whites' neighborhood by myself?

What real assurance have I that my children will be safe if I go along with this "forced" busing into the white school?

Even with all these comments from concerned black parents, the strongest opponents to busing for integration are whites not blacks, and it has its roots in tradition, misunderstandings and fear. The black parents react to these sentiments by protests. Many black parents see integrated schools as good, but are fearful of what might befall their children in some white neighborhoods where the schools are located. White parents also worry about their children going to school in a black neighborhood. They sometimes protest that busing white children to black schools means a lesser education for their children.

## "Community Control"

The idea of "black teachers teaching only black students" has arisen in recent years from a decided awareness on the part of many black people, of the poor quality of education their children were receiving in the established school system. Many believe that black teachers might have more of an interest in the children and more of an obligation to the black community in which they live than the white teacher who lives elsewhere. But probably most black parents are aware of and have taken into account the fact that there are many dedicated white teachers who are anxious to do, and have done, a good job in teaching black as well as white students.

Some black parents have been turned off by the attitude of certain impatient teachers and have been made to feel inferior and unsure of themselves. Some have discovered that they feel at a loss in communicating with their child's teacher. They do not want the child to view them as failures themselves. They, therefore, stay away and hope the child makes it.

But some black parents are very interested in what goes on at the school and make it a point to visit with their child's teacher whether the teacher has requested it or not. Other black parents may be just as interested as those who are often seen in the school, but various combinations of circumstances make it next to impossible for them to appear except in a crisis. They rightly resent the implication that they are not as interested in their children as anyone else.

One black parent stated: "I want Walter's teacher to know that I'm available and that I want to know right away if he isn't making the progress he should, so that I can correct him right then and there." There are some parents who will show quick interest in what is going on with their children, others who will be slow to respond, and still others who may never show up unless some disaster has taken place but who then may blame the teacher for not informing them sooner. But the majority of parents are interested in their children's welfare and will come to talk things over with the teacher.

An angry black parent is no different than an angry white one, and a teacher will have to be able to justify the discipline used as regards the infraction of the student. The teacher has to listen to the parent and be able to relate the circumstances leading to the punishment. Speaking of the positive incidents in the student's demeanor and school work will assure the parent that all is not lost as concerns his child. The parent must be made to realize that he is as much a part of the school as is the teacher and the student, that the parent and teaching working together can form an ideal partnership in helping the students toward a relatively successful future.

# NINE

# WHITE TEACHER...
# BLACK STUDENT

*"Don't slip me in the dozens," said Simple, "or I will tell you on which side you are related yourself. There would have to be some crossbreeding some where. I am talking about the MAN . . . "* Some Black English from Langston Hughes' short story, "Uncle Sam," in *Simple's Uncle Sam.*

Why do black kids seem to be louder and more boisterous than the same size group of white kids? How can we get black kids to deal more constructively with day-to-day frustrations of attending school? Why do black kids in the "poor" black schools (in which I teach) rip each other off rather than help each other? Should black children be forced to learn standard English? When more blacks enter the white schools what should be the teachers' attitude toward conventional speech, manners, and other middle-class values? What might we do to be effective in motivating black students? If more black students enter our schools in the next couple of years, will this mean a change in the overall behavior of the students in the school? Will we need to add courses for the students in our secondary curriculum? Why do some black unmarried teenagers think it's so great to become pregnant? Why do their friends envy them? How many black kids really respond to all this "soul" business of their own volition? How can I talk about prejudice and discrimination toward blacks in a class with only one or two black students? How do I avoid the feeling that I am hurting them or coming down on them (putting them down)? Is there an attitude today on the part of many young blacks that birth control is a form of genocide (as applied to their own race)?

### Frustrations

One of the biggest frustrations kids can experience in their school lives, from kindergarten on through school, is teacher dissapproval.

This frustration is strongest in the beginning school years, because the teacher becomes a second mother or father and "knows" *everything*. Thus the teacher's approval is very important. As children grow older, they become more aware of other affective areas outside the teacher, such as approval of their peers, broken friendships, not understanding certain school assignments and not being able to explain what the misunderstanding is. Black youngsters may also become aware that certain teachers give white students breaks, but "go-by-the-book" as far as black students are concerned. They may experience the feeling of never seeming to be able to please the teacher.

Just growing up brings natural frustrations. White teachers, as well as black, must deal with these frustrations by realizing that they are there, realizing that they go across the board of white and black, and then preparing the black as well as the white child as thoroughly as possible to meet the various frustrations and the challenges of the world. The white teacher (and the black) should become involved with students to the degree that skin color is forgotten. One wonders why model school situations such as depicted in the excellent television series "Room 222" cannot be the rule.

Probably the teacher should learn to be, as the students sometimes put it, "hard but fair"; and not worry too much that this or that student may or may not like him or her. If the teacher is consistent in student guidance in the classroom or school situation, students will normally show respect. They will exhibit an awareness that "you can't get away with that with him or her!" In some situations, teachers may be hindered in giving needed attention to students because of school conditions, e.g. overcrowding and lack of equipment, supplies, and funds for extra-curricular activities. In such instances, teachers will need to work through their professional associations to convince the community to make provisions for adequate working conditions.

It is universal among young people that at some time or other they cannot see day to day school experience as being one of the most important things in their lives. Frequently, there seems to be so many more interesting things going on. Teachers fight the battle against boredome everyday. The teacher will be better equipped if he determines precisely just what it is he wants from his students; and then works out a plan toward his goal.

Sometimes, the goals of the educational process can be distorted beyond recognition in the conflict between frustrations of a student on the one hand and frustrations of a teacher on the other. This would seem to be the case in the following incident:

A young black woman related she was on the verge of dropping out of school when she was 17. She felt she did not look as attractive as many of the other girls, had few friends, stayed home from school frequently, was barely making passing grades, and needed to make up some courses. About this time, the girl was introduced by one of her friends to an interracial club of young people. The club held "socials," went to movies, plays, museums, etc. She began to gain confidence in herself, decided she wanted to graduate from high school, and perhaps even go on to college. She went to the school counselor who encouraged her and had her assigned to a beginning typing class which was a needed make-up course.

Then the young woman went on to relate:

> I started practicing my typing at home every night . . . so that I would get an 'A' . . . When we began to practice typing on the keyboard, you had to go by slow rhythm, and I felt good because I already had got some speed, but I went slow too. The next week, the teacher called me up to the front of the room and asked me if I had taken typing before, and when I told her no, she sent me back to my seat. After that, she started watching me. I thought she was proud of me. Then, one day while the class was typing, she yelled for everyone to stop. She told me I was a liar, that I had had typing before and to get out of her class. I said I didn't lie and that I wasn't going because my counselor had given me this class. She got real mad and went out of the room and the next thing I saw was the principal coming in real mad. They told me to go to the office. When I got there I had to wait a long time and then the principal told me I was 17 and they didn't have to keep me in that school anymore and they put me out. I didn't get to graduate.

She was asked if she told the counselor what happened or her mother or the club . . . Her reply was that she hadn't because she was too ashamed.

# PERSPECTIVES ON EDUCATION AND LEARNING

An older black woman remembers the following incident from her grade school days:

> The teacher gave us an assignment to write a story in the classroom, while she did some other work. I sat there and no idea would come. Finally, when the time was about half over, I began to write a really funny story. It was all about how people act when they have to stand in line for something. Because I was writing in a hurry, I half wrote words, ran lines through things, but when I finished, I knew the teacher would like it. I got some fresh paper and started to copy it all over, but halfway through, the teacher called "time." When I tried to tell her I just wanted to copy my paper over, she wouldn't let me tell her anything and insisted on collecting my sloppy paper. A week later, she called out our names and the grades we earned for those stories. Mine was first and the only paper she read. After she had read my story, she said it was good and funny, but gave me a "zero" for the entire story, because it was sloppy. I still hate her.

Though these incidents involved white teachers and black students, black students most probably have also run up against the same kind of treatment from some black teachers. However, both these students felt they were treated as they were because they were black and the teacher white.

Students need some built-in successes, along the route the teacher has prepared. When these successes are lacking, black and white students sometimes find it easy to "turn off" the teacher, the school and, without their knowing it, their future. Some students do this because the frustration of *expected* failure is too much. The teacher needs to make clear to the student in day to day contact that the teacher cares, that he is concerned that the youngster's school-life be as successful as possible.

## Thinking Clearly

It would be helpful to teachers, and all of us, to make the effort, as much as possible, to think in terms of inductive logic; rather than in terms of generalized syllogisms. This can be accomplished fairly easily by keeping the word "some" in the forefront of our minds instead of the word "all." It often can be inferred from a question that the premise of the question is an unstated "all" syllogism.

From the question, for instance, why are groups of black young people more boisterous than groups of white young people we can infer the thought process: All black youngsters are more boisterous than white youngsters; there is a group of black youngsters; therefore they are more boisterous than whites. This type of "all" reasoning tends to preclude further investigation or study of a problem and hence dealing with the problem (if it is determined it should be dealt with). Relying on observations and induction one would think thusly: Some groups of black young people, or the black people I've observed, are boisterous. This would then probably bring to mind that some groups of white young people, one has observed, are also boisterous. One then might be led to the consideration of the specific conditions giving rise to boisterous behavior; of where, when, and why it occurs. Are black youngsters, for instance, any more "boisterous" than those whites who storm a football field, tear down the goal posts and rampage through a town or neighborhood? Are black youngsters worse behaved than those white youngsters who engage in riotous behavior at rock festivals, etc?

A sixteen year old black high school student related what she observed as a child when she would go with her mother to department stores. She said, she'd see white kids running around, getting under dress racks, behind counters, yelling to each other and having fun. Her mother would not allow her to do this, would make her sit or just stand, and give her looks designed to make her behave. She went on to say:

> . . . last week, I went downtown and I saw a black mother with her little girl in one of the department stores. The little girl was running around, looking at everything, talking loud, picking up toys, and running under dress racks while her mother paid no attention to her. At first I got mad when I saw how the little black girl behaved, but then I started to remember how I felt when I saw the white

kids do just what she was doing, and I felt free. I didn't know why I felt free, but I felt like a big load was lifted from my chest, because black kids could do what white kids could do and nothing bad would happen to them, because there wasn't any difference.

There may be a number of aspects to the girl's feeling "free" after this incident; but one is that she became able to look at things as they are, to note that some white children and some black children behave the same; and she was no longer bound by the stereotype that blacks behave worse than whites.

In many ghetto schools there is, to be sure, a great deal of "ripping off" behavior, but there is also some "helping" behavior. A group of black high school students in the ghetto expressed themselves this way on these subjects:

Black kids don't always fight each other and when they do it's because they live in different neighborhoods or different buildings and have 'turf' they want to protect. Or sometimes there's a gang and they want money, so they take it off some other kids that don't belong in the gang. Sometimes (put in another kid) they don't even know each other and they decide they don't like each other and they fight. After that they might get to know and like each other."

These students said they would like teachers (white and black) to know that they do help each other, but that adults never talk about the good things, just about the rumbles that happen. One student gave an example of trying to help another:

. . . one time one of the dudes missed an English test, because there was some trouble at home; and, in front of the class, the teacher, who is white, said that the kids on ADC (Aid to Dependent Children) always stay home, especially when there was a test. And that our friend was going to fail. We knew that if he failed he wouldn't graduate, so after class we tried to talk it out with the teacher to see if she'd give the dude another chance. But she was mad and asked us if we were his lawyers and that she ran the class. Then we went over to see him after school and told him what had happened. He said he wasn't on ADC and that the teacher was a liar. But after that he was too ashamed and wouldn't come to class and he didn't graduate, just dropped out of school.

White teachers sometimes ask why black kids seem to want to hurt or embarass one another by name-calling, especially using the derogatory term "nigger." One of the students answered in this way:

If another dude calls me 'nigger' and I know him; well, I know he's just kidding me and I laugh and call him 'nigger' back.

When the students were asked if they felt the word "nigger" was a "bad" word or term, they replied to the effect that "in the olden days" it was a real "put down" and black people "couldn't handle it," and would fight anybody if they were called that name; but that now "nigger" doesn't mean anything to young people. "We're black and beautiful and they can't hurt us with that anymore . . . even Dick Gregory used 'nigger' as the title of his book." When asked, since they felt that way, if a white person could now call them "nigger" without their getting angry, they quickly and loudly replied, "They'd better not!", that when they (the blacks) used it among themselves, they understood and it was not the same when somebody white tried it. However, they seemed to agree that if a "white dude" who was a close friend used the word, and didn't get "up-tight" if they called him "honky," "dago," or "kike," then "no sweat."

Black students have stated that when in integrated situations, higher tolerance and grades seem to go to the white students. Black students, they say, are regarded as trouble-makers if they protest or bring too much attention to themselves in the classroom or school.

These things can happen because the teacher is or may be frustrated through past prejudices or ignorance in understanding the black students' problems. Teachers may seek guidelines from those teachers nearby who are experiencing the same problems. But they may be unable to give help. The teacher, finding no solutions or guidelines, may fall back upon old prejudices and beliefs and the problems increase. Teachers cannot begin to lessen the day-to-day frustrations of students if they themselves continue to be frustrated because of prejudice. Hopefully, this book will provide some aid in dealing with problems of desegregation.

## Blacks' English

It is a fact that most black children born in the United States of America after growing-up are going to have to find employment in order to have at least the bare necessities of life. In order to compete in the job market, they are going to have to do so on every level, and successfully if they want to work.

One of the basic requirements is that they be able to both read and understand a job application one that is written in "standard" English. After reading and understanding the application, they must fill it out using "standard" English spelling, so that whoever reads it, can understand what has been written. After they have read, understood, and filled it out in "standard" English, they must then converse in "standard" English so that the potential or future employer knows that when certain orders are relayed to the employee, he will understand what is being said, meant and expected of him. When he reports back as to whether or not the job has been finished, he must do so in "standard" English so that he will be understood and/or helped.

There is no such thing as "bad" or "good" English, only educated and uneducated. Black people come from just about every part of our country and they speak with an eastern, southern, western, mid-western, and northern sound, just as do their white counterparts. And mixed into those "sounds" are words like "ax" for "ask"; "mellin' " for "meddling"; "done" for "did"; "hope" for "wish"; "done did it" for "has done it"; chopped off or added endings; words switched around; sometimes speaking so rapidly that words run together; or so slowly that words become distorted. And sometimes tacked on to all of that, the exciting use of "slang" which catches on so quickly, that folks who claim to only use "standard" English find themselves occasionally using "black" slang.

162

Black people of all economic classes speak English which is perfectly comprehensible to anyone else speaking English. The overwhelming majority of blacks do not, in their normal everyday conversations, speak in some arcane jargon understood only by those with dark skins and/or Negroid features. So-called "Black English" can also be found spoken among some Southern whites.

Advocates for perpetuating so-called "Black English" among poor black children do not seem secure enough to similarly advocate the use of "White English" among poor white children. In other words, they do not suggest that "youse" for "you"; "hyah" for "here"; "irregardless" for "regardless"; "pint" for "point"; "toin" for "turn"; "de" for "the"; "doze" for "those", is "White English" and therefore should be taught to all poor white children. Whites usually regard these examples as uneducated English to be corrected for social and business success in the student's future. If this is true, then it stands to reason that teaching of "Black English" and "White English" will be of little value against reaching "standard" English. Teachers, black or white, should understand this and see that their students are grounded in, what the system regards as one of its keys to success, "standard" English.

Perhaps teachers cannot hope to go into the homes of their students in order to change the English patterns of their parents if "poor" or uneducated English is to be found therein. But that must not be a deterrent in making sure that the students understand and learn to use "standard" English right along with the "home or neighborhood English." While there is nothing to be ashamed of or lost in learning to use the kind of English that will help open doors of opportunity for the questing individual, there likewise need be no shame regarding the use of "poor" or uneducated English. Both educated and uneducated English are a means of communication. Where one will not work, the other sometimes will.

A white teacher who has been teaching black students for some time remarked:

I can understand my black students, but when other whites say they cannot understand the speech of black people and ask how I can, I am at a loss to be able to tell them how I understand them. What can I say?

163

This is proof of how strong stereotypic ideas can be and how they can confuse clear thought on a simple fact so thoroughly that the person involved cannot even attempt to answer this kind of question without help. The fact is that the black students are speaking English, not a foreign language, not a deep dark dialect, baffling to the sensitive white ear. The teacher understands the students because he and they speak a mutual language, English! While it is true that young people are sometimes more colorful in their use of English, it is nevertheless basically the same sound patterns that the white teacher has learned too. But because he expects that he should *not* be able to understand them (the blacks), he is baffled because he does.

One of the bulwarks of segregation and prejudice is that black people are "bad," different from whites, that white people cannot understand either the intricacies of the black mind or speech, that therefore it is much wiser and better to remain socially apart. And in order that segregation continues, there must be constant subtle and conspicuous reminders to that effect.

The white teacher who posed the question, how do I understand them, was half-held by reminders of expectations of white inability to understand blacks." He found himself unable to carry through logically on the proven fact that he could and did understand the speech of the students and other black people with whom he came into contact. He could have answered the question, "How can you understand black people, if other white people can't?" with "The black students I have talked to are American and speak English, and if you'd like to meet and talk with them, come along. As we converse I am sure you will find they use the same language as you." Instead, he was so conditioned that he thought it strange that he could understand what blacks were saying, too!

## Values and Manners

Black students entering white schools for the first time are, for the most part, looking for the same educational standards and experiences afforded the white student. Most black students have already experienced in some way over-crowded schools and poor neighborhood surroundings. They are hoping to matriculate in a middle-class school with competent and understanding teachers, and friendly students as well. The white teacher's attitude should be simply one of making sure that *all* the students in the class receive adequate educational attention.

Manners may be conceived of as "little laws" designed to keep conflict and chaos out of our daily lives. For example, "Thank you," "Excuse me," "I'm sorry," "Please," "May I," "After you," "If you please," are all designed to keep "feathers unruffled." It is difficult to stay angry when someone steps on your foot, or causes you to drop your books all over the corridor, if the words "I'm so sorry," or "Please let me help you pick those books up" are heard.

Black children from black homes are not strangers to good manners, but sometimes "bad manners" have become a protection for them in the neighborhoods where they live. Here is an example: In a poor black neighborhood where gangs may roam, there usually is a lot of standing around on street corners by fellows with obviously nothing else to do and one person accidentally bumps into another. "I'm sorry to have bumped into you, please excuse me," says the "Bumper" to the "Bumpee." The "Bumpee" may hear something else in the "Bumpers" request for forgiveness, other than "good manners"; he may hear a "clanging weakness" which means he can now "show off" to his street corner buddies without fear of retribution from the "weaker" one. So his reply may range from calling the "Bumper" some classic dirty names to punching the "Bumper" in the mouth. So therefore the black students coming from this environment may view "bad manners" as a natural protection against any insult or physical violence.

The white or black teacher needs to understand this in the very beginning and not appear to get very angry if a student displays the kind of behavior that indicates "bad" manners. The endeavor of the teacher should be toward helping the student understand when and where "good" manners will bring positive results rather than negative ones. He may need the "bad" manners that experience has taught him is valid, to be able to survive in the kind of community that regards "good" manners as strange and vulnerable. This, however, does not mean the student is unaware of "good" manners or even that he does not use them at home or in the community. It is simply that many children are in the street much of the time and use all the knowledge they have learned there to survive. It is natural that coming to a strange place which may be filled with "hostile" strangers, they will sometimes exhibit the manner of protection they have learned so well.

"Lower class" values and "middle class" values both serve a similar purpose — that of protecting the individual in the environment in which he lives, works and plays. They are "get along" guidelines, and when they are violated, a penalty of some sort is levied against the violator. This does not mean that the values of both "lower-or-middle class" cannot be understood and implemented by people of either class. Values are learned by trial and error, and young people need to know alternate ways of behavior in order to succeed in this world. They need to understand that it is not a "put down" for some to live "on this side of the tracks . . . while some live on the other." They should know the requirements of both sides, and imparting information or creating a zest for knowledge *is* the role of the teacher in our society.

Some white teachers who have never taught black students wonder if they must lower their values in order to "get along" with the black students in their classes. An effective teacher cannot afford to merely "get along" with a student. All students, black or white, have the right to get a clear understanding of what their role as student is and what the role of the teacher really is. "Getting along" is fine, but it is a peripheral plus.

A teacher cannot be afraid of students and do a good job of sharing knowledge. Students will sense the fear, and some will take advantage of it. At the same time they may resent the teacher and what the fear infers — that they are less then human and will react to that inference. This reaction can manifest itself in many ways, not studying, hostile words or looks, ignoring the teachers requests, cutting classes and so on. When students first enter a class, they overtly or covertly "size up" the teacher. The teacher should be aware of this and, in turn, should be "sizing up" the class. The teacher should be thinking of ways to communicate that he or she is there to help the students learn and will be accessible. Remarks such as "*Before* you came here we . . ." "My *former* students didn't . . ." "I want you to behave just like my old students . . ." and so on, should be avoided.

"Getting personal" with a student about his family and family style is something to be approached carefully, and only after a basis of trust has been clearly established. Also, the teacher should be discreet in the use of any information he obtains regarding a student's family life. For instance, in one school a student told his counselor, after being reprimanded for disrespectful behavior toward his homeroom teacher, that the teacher was always asking about his family and whether or not his father lived with them. The teacher had meant to be helpful. However, in his quest for more information, he confided in other teachers, who had contact with the student, of conversations the student thought were in confidence. The student learned of this and became very angry. A trust was broken . . . "You can't trust whites." Black students, like white students, will sometimes find a teacher whom they can admire and treat as a confidant, who will have great influence on the student's educational growth, and perhaps even their social growth . . . but only if trust is established and maintained.

## Inspiring (Motivating) Students

Teachers cannot hope to give every student the same kind of concentrated effort. But they can share their own sense of inner security, their own zest for what they are doing, and their own interest in the fates of their students. Many times teachers never get to know which student, or how many students were encouraged to attempt something they had before thought impossible and succeeding at it. A white high school teacher in a Northern Illinois school relates she received a letter of thanks, along with a photostatic copy of a medical degree, from a southern university granted to one of her former black students. She had not heard from him in twelve years. When he had first entered her class in a predominantly white school, he was somewhat sullen and withdrawn. She began talking to him, found he was quite bright, visited his mother and father (who were poor and had nine other children), and through various means of encouragement helped him benefit from his school attendance.

Mrs. Jewel Careathers, a second grade teacher at Denver's Stedman Elementary School shows pupils bused in to achieve integration in the predominatly black school January 31, 1972 where to sit. The integration was achieved without incident.          (UPI Photo)

## The Changing School

Many teachers facing the fact that black students will soon be joining white students in their schools for the first time are wondering and worrying whether or not behavior of the student body will disintegrate into chaos and confusion. Some teachers also seem to feel a hopelessness in their ability to help make the experience a positive one. They find it hard to view the whole thing as a "moving ahead" bursting with exciting possibilities, of helping to bring together a society which has long been split because of racial animosities.

Black and white students wonder about each other, because the young are naturally curious, and because much has been said both pro and con regarding each other. Some of the students on both sides look forward to the experience, in a positive fashion. Some don't care one way or the other. Some face it with trepidation. Still others view the situation with hatred and hold a desire to hurt one another — physically, mentally or both.

Teachers have to face and understand these varying moods. They need to help prepare students, both black and white — those preparing to attend and those awaiting the event — by discussing the positives of an open school. Students need to understand that every child has a right to attend a school without harassment, that the time to learn about each other and their various roles in further developing this country together in harmony is *now* and the place provided for such intellectual growth is in the schools.

Students, regardless of color, need to understand that infraction of school rules by any students, will be fairly dealt with, that any infraction based on racial animosity will be squarely and swiftly dealt with so that peaceful and uninterrupted learning can proceed.

Unfortunately, the change that is most often seen is the abrupt departure of white students to other schools when blacks begin entering, causing the particular school to become either a black majority or all black; and that is too bad. It is too bad because these students will have lost the opportunity to discover that there are good things to learn about each other and positive paths to be taken together in helping the country overcome one of its largest, persistent and pernicious problems, racial prejudice.

The addition of a human relations course to the curriculum is desirable, because students from elementary through postsecondary schools of black and white backgrounds are very curious about one another, and are very vocal about it. It must be the kind of course that bridges hostility with understanding based on well-substantiated facts, using Black History as reference material. It must pave the way for honest and open communication without fear of ridicule or retribution. The course should examine prejudice for what it really is; how it really starts, why it has been needed by some, who needed it, what it was meant to do; whether or not it succeeded, and what today's results are. The goal must be to smooth the way to a peaceful and lasting lessening of racial tensions within and without the school.

It must take into account the very real fact of emotion rather than logic playing a huge part in racial conflict. Here is an emotional example from a graduate student working toward a teaching certificate:

> My grandmother whom I love dearly told me that black people were little bitches and sires, who only grieved a short time for their missing pups, and during the course of time forgot all about them. The black parents are the same way, even if they keep the children, and the proof is that they don't care what they do in school or even if they go, or not, as long as they are out of the house and out of sight.

When the student was confronted with some facts contradicting her grandmother's opinion, she retorted angrily, "Don't attack *my* grandmother!"

The secondary curriculum may have to add some remedial reading courses, depending on the educational background of the students newly entering the school. It may also have to add accelerated courses. The purpose of the educational system is to help students gain a better understanding of the world about them, and whatever needs to be added to achieve this goal is desirable.

## Needs and Responsibilities

Sex and the teenager is the stuff of many books, movies, and speculation, most of them heretofore involving whites. Most teenage girls, as well as boys, dream of the day they can be on their own: no parents to nag, no responsibilities other than those they wish, no restriction on how late they stay up, on what and when they eat. In short, they believe adulthood to be a glorious state. Black teenagers are no exception.

Movies, books, televisions, plays and commercials sing of the bliss of being a young married. The teens watch the young married opening their brand new refrigerators, driving spanking new automobiles, either happily walking or running to meet the dream man or woman while etheral music pours forth, watching the wife or husband wash their hair with some bubbly concoction while the mate companionably walks in surprised at how smart the wife or husband is, and later whispering beautiful compliments in the shell-like ear.

The girls are treated to such scenes as a young mother holding a beautiful baby. Another young mother extols the virtues of some baby product while drooling over the baby. The husband is usually just out of earshot or later is seen smiling fondly at his wife and child. There are many young girls who dream of just such a life. Because of the relative innocence of youth, they unwittingly block out reality and logic and believe that the Prince Charming of their day-dreams is the guy who lives next door, or is in the same classroom, or a guy just met at some dance or other.

The fellow, on the other hand, may be the same age as the girl in question or an older guy looking for a quick conquest. But all are essentially looking for the same thing, love, acceptance, and independence. Since it is almost impossible to really find all three of these wants rolled into one, disaster may lurk just around the corner.

The girl has a baby, does or does not marry, but in either event now has to work to help take care of the baby or joins the ADC rolls so she and the baby can live.

These things happen to white girls as well as black girls. Most black girls do not think that it is great to become pregnant, but some think that becoming pregnant will force the fellow to marry them. Others may become pregnant because they have a strong wish for something of their own to love and take care of. They feel that it is the only safe love there is. Still others have little knowledge of birth control measures, the alternatives of abortion or the avenues of adoption.

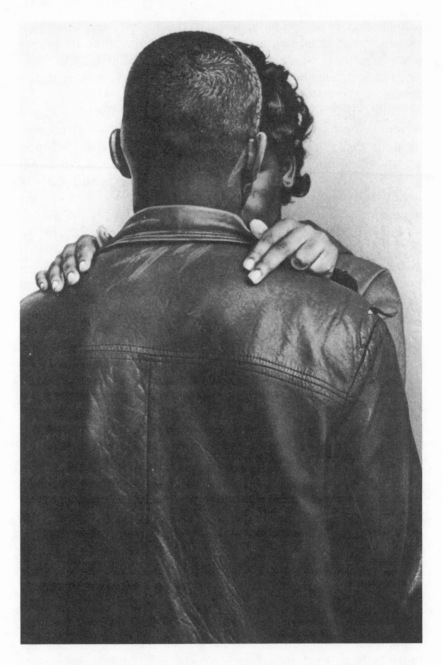

*Staircases of 16-story project hi-rises are seldom used except by teenagers seeking privacy.* (Chicago Daily News Photo)

The question "Why do their friends envy them?" can best be answered thusly: Isn't it the most natural thing when confronted by a brand new baby to hear yourself saying, "My that's a beautiful baby, how I envy you." Saying this does not really mean you envy them and want to go out and conceive a baby yourself, but that you appreciate the fact that babies are wonderful. It is natural to think that a baby is fulfilling to any normal woman. To not wish aloud that one had just such a beautiful baby would be regarded as either being jealous or as being a bit strange.

There is a social need of all human beings to be able to identify with some segment of society, and "soul" is understood by just about every black in America or abroad. Individual black students do not agree on every point as to personal life style, commitments, attitudes, and ideas under the "soul" banner. But they do agree that "soul" understanding makes it possible to go to a strange city, school, or gathering and almost immediately become comfortable if another black is present, stranger or not.

The "soul" understanding works the same magic for a solitary Irishman in a roomful of Englishmen who suddenly becomes aware that another Irishman has just entered by either the sound of his voice, or some statement that marks him as a son of Erin. Soul is a kind of lovely acceptance offered from one human being to another, whether white or black.

Teachers, by way of their profession, can certainly speak of prejudice and discrimination toward blacks without feeling that they are bruising the feelings of the black students if they (the teachers) have full understanding of the subject and some clear thoughts on some solutions to these prejudices. The black students will feel relieved and proud to discover that their teacher has the ability to lay the ghost of prejudice and hatred to rest with common sense conversation along with questions and answers.

The only time a teacher or anyone else might feel guilty of putting down a student during such discussion is if they believe the prejudices themselves. So the teacher must first work hard to understand what he feels himself and then to discover ways of presenting answers and new forms of behavior in the classroom.

There are some blacks who apparently believe there is a very real plan to eliminate the "black" problem by a conspiracy of "black" birth control resulting in genocide. The fear is that as the older people die there will be no young to step in their place, thereby effectively eliminating the black race . . . They cite the plans of Hitler to eliminate the Jewish people from the face of the earth which nearly succeeded, and instances of forced sterilization which have been practiced by some welfare agencies in this country.

Young black militants have taken up this cry and urge that black women pay no attention to the warnings of overpopulation as stated by the white system. Here is an example of what one young black high school student stated:

> If I become pregnant, I'm not going to get rid of it, because I don't believe in destroying life. Besides, I will be helping my people to survive.

The young girl is one of nine children living with her mother and father in a low rent project.

And, from a young black male high school student:

> I don't want to start a family until I graduate from college, but if anything would happen, I would be against my girl having an abortion. I won't kill my own to help the white establishment.

### Counselors

Black students from time to time mention a general distrust of white counselors in high schools, colleges and universities. They feel that counselors should be willing to share all the helpful information they have on hand and be willing to gather new information for the student when needed. But experience has shown that prejudice and sterotyping can even be found in the office of the counselor.

For instance, a black student attending a vocational high school decided in his second year that he wanted to become a dentist. After thinking it over, he talked to his parents and convinced them that he was serious about what he wanted to do. They in turn took him to visit a dentist and they knew to discuss the pros and cons of such a venture. The dentist was so impressed with the student's earnestness that he pledged partial sponsorship in college, if the student graduated from high school with a high average and if he maintained a high average in college.

The next week the student and his mother visited the school counselor, who was white, and discussed the matter of transferring to another school so that he could pick up classes in the biological sciences. The counselor told both the mother and the student that they were only wasting time, that he had heard all of this before, that it was his experience that kids with such ideas sooner or later dropped out of school. He went on to say that a lot of these kids get these kinds of ideas because they have to find an excuse as to why they are not doing as well as they should. They then get everyone excited and then "cop out." His advice was that the student forget about being a dentist, that he could help him become a good auto mechanic, and that is what he (the student) should really buckle down to.

The mother sent her son out so that she could speak to the counselor in private. She had expected that the counselor would further encourage her son to really work hard toward achieving the goals he had set for himself, not to totally discourage him. When she tearfully informed the counselor of her expectations, he replied that he "knew" these students and he "knew" her son. There was no way that he could be a dentist or anything else in that direction, but he was pretty good with his hands. He stated he would not recommend a transfer and that as far as he (the counselor) was concerned the vocational school was the best thing for her son. He concluded that most students coming to a vocational school were potential drop-outs anyway, thus a failure wouldn't cost his family that much money.

Black counselors in predominantly white schools complain that many white counselors will discuss problems of black students with anyone who will listen, but are very reticent about discussing problems of white students outside their offices. The black counselors also state that some white counselors behave as though the problems of black students are so different from white that they must have a black counselor's serious and studied advice, only to learn later that this sought-after advice is never used.

Counselors are very important because they are "trouble-shooters" before the students' "problems" get out of hand.

Counselors can aid students to develop new ways of looking at problems. Counselors are the pillars standing between a wrong and right student-made decision. A counselor acts as the student's friend in court so-to-speak, helping the student to find his way in the maze of academic and social trivia that daily beset him. Should a student get into trouble with a teacher, another student, or things are not quite right at home and prevent him from being able to cope, there should stand the counselor. And color should have absolutely nothing to do with it. But if color does make a difference, it means that the counselor likely needs the help of a race relations course in order to help himself function better as a helper of students in the fullest sense. After such a course, he may be capable of helping other counselors struggling with the chauvinism of race. Black students present the same problems as do white students, pretty much across the board. Prejudicial views of the past, however, continue to fog the facts while underscoring the great myth of substantial differences between blacks and whites.

Counselors should understand and appreciate the various cultural backgrounds from which black and white students come. But they should also understand that in terms of our American cultural system all young people are more alike than they are different.

Black students do not have ancient and strange black ways of looking at and practicing life anymore than Irish students practice ancient Druid rites.

Counselors are human too, and sometimes they may forget how encouraging or damaging they can be to a student in pointing out certain directions. They should attempt to understand in their own minds and hearts what it is they wish ultimately to happen to the student with whom they are working.

### Teacher—Teacher Relationships

A few words may be in order at this point concerning black-white teacher relationships.

A black teacher was assigned to a certain high school and found that he was the only black teacher in the school. He discovered that the only time, after the first day, that the white teachers would really talk to him was when complaining about a black student or asking for some "black" advice on a "black" problem.

When he would go to lunch in the faculty lunch room, he always felt that he was intruding or breaking up a private conversation. He was either talked to, or talked at, or after a time, simply ignored. Finally he began eating his lunch in his classroom and nobody asked him why.

Later in talking with some of the white teachers, he found that they had felt too embarrassed to talk to him, for fear they would say something "racially insulting" without even meaning to. They took his quietness for censure and wondered how to talk to him, how to make friends with him. They finally gave up until one of them heard from some white students what the black students had to say of the white teachers' "ill treatment" of the black teacher. It was then they decided to have a real "communication-fest" with him and the above was what came of their conversation.

Clear communication is a must for teachers and indeed any personnel directly or indirectly involved with students whether young or old. Race relations seminars can do much toward opening more and more doors of understanding between people.

In the integrated school situation, whether majority white or black, teachers sometimes worry about facing hostility from each other based on racial animosity. They wonder how to cope, to convince those with hostile feelings that they are not the enemy, that they take the position of teaching very seriously. An example of this quandary is expressed by a white teacher already teaching in a majority black school who has been unable to break the barrier of distrust and animosity displayed by some of the black teachers:

> How can I, as a white teacher, say and do the right things
> to be accepted by the black teachers in this school, not
> only as a dedicated colleague, but as a potential friend
> as well?

This is the kind of question some white teachers about to enter a school on a full time basis ask in contemplating working with black teachers for the first time. There never is an easy C follows B, B follows A, kind of answer. Most people suffer these same kinds of anxieties whenever they are about to meet new people, regardless of race, or ethnic origin.

The giving of advice is always hazardous. However some teachers have advised that they feel the following list of suggestions can be of some use:

It may be best not to

a) try to convince anyone of your sincerity in coming to a ghetto school; quite simply, actions speak better than words;

b) air your views about how poorly black youngsters are being taught (especially at the beginning); the reaction of your listeners may be "Well, here comes another 'know-nothinger' telling *us* the problem!" "What took you so long?"

c) show surprise when you find that a black teacher living and teaching in the ghetto is politically, socially and culturally informed;

d) tell about how well a certain student is doing in your class, and how poorly he does in others; you would be giving jealousy a chance to rear its ugly head, and could mean trouble by creating unnecessary hostility toward your own work;

e) allow yourself to become part of a clique; try to steer clear and draw your own conclusions from your own observations;

f) enter into a discussion that sounds as if someone's being "panned"; your part in such a conversation, when repeated by others, may seem to have been the only part;

g) repeat anything you have heard from one person about another, (unless it is something good);

h) try to convince anyone that you are friendly; many times (to quote an old adage) friendliness is mistaken for weakness, and you really do not need *that* kind of confusion;

i) laugh too loudly or too long at another's joke; if you find that you are laughing alone you'll be embarrassed, as will the teller of the joke, and embarrassment usually turns into anger, or dislike (if it's very funny to you, however, then have a ball, but don't be apologetic because you alone found it so.)

It is problaby best just to be one's self, not letting role-playing interfere with natural warmth in inter-personal relations with colleagues. One should not fall into the pit of feeling one must like every teacher working in the same school. People are, after all, just people. Some you will like, some you will not.

### The Substitute Teacher

One more word, this time touching on the Substitute Teacher Syndrome, that is the plight of the teacher who finds himself or herself on call wherever needed at whatever time.

There is a basic security in knowing most of the time that we have a specially assigned place that we know is mostly unchanging. We can get settled and perhaps proceed at an orderly rate within an orderly schedule. If we are teachers, then our students know us and give us some measure of respect; and we know the students, what their expectations are and what we can do toward sharing helpful information with them.

However, substitute teachers can suffer a. form of paranoia or self-doubt. Students often view the substitute teacher as fair game; not as a substitute for their teaching missing for a day or two or four. The students usually believe that no matter what they do, the teacher cannot "get even" because they will never see her or him again. It is also found that that students' academic or social background, or race, have nothing to do with this attitude. It almost seems as if students absorb this philosophy through a strange kind of osmosis.

Usually the "sub" doesn't know the teacher she is temporarily standing in for or what the last assignment was, or what the regular teacher's technique in teaching is. Sometimes the sub does not even know how long he or she will be there. As one substitute teacher put it:

> After "subbing" for a year, I finally worked out a solution. If the teacher has left an assignment, I get the students to do it by appointing the most aggressive student as my assistant. If there is no prepared assignment, I ask the students what the hardest assignment they have had that

semester and offer my help with the problems they couldn't solve. Both of those techniques usually get their attention. However, if they won't listen at all, I pull out a book or send for the principal. But, I never let myself feel defeated or useless. I just try to work harder on the next job I have.

Perhaps doing your "own thing", something you're really sure of for the time or day you are in the classroom is best, especially if class work is out of the question. Outside of regular class work, there is absolutely nothing like a short race relations class. The "sub" need not be an expert, but can talk about how prejudice grows and why it still is uppermost in many peoples' minds. In addition, the students can be encouraged to state their views, their thoughts, or solutions.

If not race relations, there is always the space program, cancer, drugs, or the goals of the individual students.

But one thing is certain, the "substitute teacher" is an important and integral part of the educational system. They are there to help when a teacher gap appears and, to move on to become the "regular" teacher who will touch many lives, and hopefully urging some students on to future greatness. The substitute teacher should never think of his job as merely a "substitution for the real thing," but as a much needed helper on the road of education for our young.

### Observations

In an essay entitled "New Teacher" by Reed Hundt, appearing in *Crisis in Urban Education* the following statement is made: "Every new teacher — certainly every new white teacher — is mentally, emotionally and physically blitzed by the experience of the black ghetto school." The author goes on to indicate that very few graduates are prepared for the job of teaching in urban school systems.

One may not be able to quarrel with these observations, but within the value premises of this book, they evoke the following responses:

**180**

For one thing, the continued existence of black ghetto schools in large Northern urban areas, often ascribed to *de facto* (but non-legal) segregation, is no more desirable than the segregated and previously legal existence of dual school systems in most of the South. And for another, the time has come for teachers, prospective teachers, and others to disenthrall themselves from the dogmas and prejudices of the past and to instead begin educating for the harmonious living together of all peoples.

Robert J. Havighurst, in an essay entitled "Requirements for A Valid 'New Criticism' " in the same *Crisis in Urban Education*, put it this way:

> I see the educational establishment reorganized and revitalized, together with the socio-political establishment. The work will largely be done by activists who learn to innovate creatively and to evaluate their innovations scientifically.

TEN

# BLACK-WHITE
# STUDENT RELATIONS

*Cats would come along with this "baby" thing . . . 'Hey,
baby, How you doin' baby?' in every phase of the Negro
hip life . . . I doubt that they're many, if any gray people
who could ever say 'baby' to a Negro and make him feel
that 'me and this cat have got something going, something
strong going." Manchild in the Promised Land,* by Claude
Brown.

I have to admit I'm afraid of black kids, they seem so sure of
themselves and quickly put you down. What can I do to overcome
my fear? I've heard that black kids' parents allow them more
freedom than we get and don't expect their kids to associate only
with kids of specially picked families; is that what makes them
different from us? I want to know the black kids like I know my
white friends; and I want to let them know I want to be friends; how
can I without seeming to be condescending? I'm in an integrated
school and I notice that there are white students friendly to the
blacks, but the blacks won't accept their friendships — why? Why
do some colored kids want to be called black, others Negro and still
others colored? How do I know who wants to be called what? I've
heard that black kids all want to put "soul food" into the school
cafeterias, is this a legitimate wish or do they just want to make
trouble? How can a white student get over prejudice if he is afraid
to talk openly with the black students for fear of hurting their
feelings and making them mad? How come in school it's o.k. to be
with black students, but at home the thought of such a thing is
terrible to your parents? Why do parents instill in their children a
fear of the black student? Do black students feel "funny" when
they are a minority in a white school? Why do black students upon
entering white schools decide on separate tables and organizations?
Do all black kids think all white kids are "honkies?" What is a
"Honky?" What can black and white students do to make things
better?

183

These are just a few of many observations and questions noted and asked by white students regarding black students who either are preparing to join them in a school, or who are there at the present time. The questions are very important because these students are trying to find a level of communication that will ease racial tensions between black and white students in the same school. For instance, the opening statement and question of this chapter has its counterpart in the black students' fears when entering a previously all-white school for the first time. Here is an example:

I was really looking forward to going to this high school, because everyone in my family said that graduating from there would mean a lot when it came to going to a good college. They told me I wouldn't have any trouble with the white kids, because they came from highly educated families and didn't look at the race problems like, maybe, a working class white would.

Like the first day wasn't too bad, they (the white students) were nice, but distant; like they didn't want to make me feel too uncomfortable. During orientation, I saw two or three more black students, but I didn't want to be too obvious and run right to them. During lunch some white kids were chosen to sit with me so I wouldn't be alone the first day. After a while of trying to talk to me and me trying to talk to them, they left me alone and just talked to each other. I felt like a fool; I wished I was anywhere but there.

After a while I began to notice a difference in the kids who joined us. They began making remarks about some people not knowing where they belonged. The white kids who were supposed to be with me, didn't say anything in my defense at all. Later, I found I hated to walk down the halls or go to the washroom alone, because I would always get bumped or if I left a book on my desk when I returned I would sometimes find a nasty note in it or a page torn out. Now I don't trust any of these white kids. I can't figure out who is really friendly and who is not and I never know what ugly thing they're going to do next. It's almost like we few black kids here are on an island that might sink any minute. My parents and friends thought that the people at this school would be different than a poor white school, but it isn't.

Schools must help students to focus on common goals rather than wallow in racial conflicts. Students must be made to realize that school is for everyone, that intimidation is not a part of the curriculum and will not be tolerated. Since most students will not report this kind of behavior, black or white, mandatory human relations workshops which explore harassment based on racial misunderstanding are a "must." Bringing things out in the open, with a clear understanding that racial animosity must first be acknowledged, is the only way of helping to correct misbehavior based on racial fears and racist attitudes.

Overcoming fear regarding blacks or whites is really an individual problem. The student has first to figure out why he fears, whether or not he has personally experienced anything fearful from the black or white student, and what good things he has either heard of or experienced in the black-white relationship. Then if he can accept the theory of the brotherhood of man and can begin to seek out friendly discussions, he is on his way out of fear. He should understand that some blacks and whites are hostile and capable of doing great harm. On the other hand, the individual must come to acknowledge that most blacks and whites are not hostile, but merely wary of accepting overtures from someone they do not know. Students, as well as adults have to be discerning in their choice of friends, no matter what one's color, religion, or nationality may happen to be. The student may not like all blacks or all whites that he meets, but that is not necessary or even expected by most people.

Black students come from all social levels, just as do their white counterparts, and most of their parents are very concerned as to who their friends are and the kinds of backgrounds they come from. Since many black people come from poor or working class families and crowded neighborhoods, some whites believe that black family life is so chaotic that the parents neither care where their children go or with whom they make friends.

However, that is not true, because most parents, whatever their racial background, have a pretty good idea of what the "wrong" companions can contribute to their child's life and will go to great pains to try to make sure their children are well protected. On the other hand, most American children, no matter of what racial or ethnic background, are gaining more and more freedom to decide for themselves what they will or will not do. In a way this shows progress for human kind. But if with all these new freedoms the young are now enjoying, some basic "filling in" regarding the world and its people are not forthcoming, then confusion due to misinformation becomes unavoidable.

## Friendships

Parental permissiveness is not what makes black kids seem different from white kids. It is the *fact* of segregation, coupled with fear, that blinds people to their sameness and perceives "differences" to be all bad, especially between black and white. Friendships must be allowed to grow without consciously pushing amid high anxiety to quickly become close buddies. Black and white friendships are not uncommon, though perhaps rarer than they should be due to a lack of propinquity. Here are the views of a young black male college student regarding black-white friendships:

I roomed with a white guy for about two years while in college and I thought we'd become good friends. We found our personalities were about the same, and we even double-dated. When I came back home, he visited my family and I would go and visit his. After we graduated, he went to work in one state, and I, in another. Whenever he would come through town, I would invite my friends over and have a small party to make him feel at home. Sometimes we would double-date, go to a really great restaurant, and I would pick up the tab. But one time I had the occasion to visit him in his city. I could only stay a couple of days, but during that time, I didn't meet one of his friends. And instead of showing me the town, he took me to some dinky little hole in the wall greasy spoon, which I'm sure he had never even seen before.

I finally got married and took my bride to meet him and got the same treatment as before. I really got the message that time, and I told him off. It was all right for him to meet my friends, but I was not good enough to meet his.

And these remarks from one of his friends standing nearby:

I personally believe through long observation that there is at least one cultural difference between white and black people. Blacks can get very angry and yell and scream out of frustration at one another and understand that it is not the end of all future friendly relationship. Black people don't always mean *everything* evil they may say in the heat of an argument, and will be able to still be friends . . . that is, *most* black people. But, it seems to me, that most white folks, on the other hand, will take an argument they are involved in with a black very seriously and will not wish to continue the friendship, even if he (the white) is wrong. Instead, he will try to finish you off in your business or hurt you in some other way . . .

On the other side of the coin, here is what a high school student has to say:

I'm graduating from high school next year and this school is mostly white. When I came here, I had heard how you couldn't trust the white kids, even those who acted friendly. So I was cool, minded my own business, and let them alone. But then I joined the basketball team along with a couple of my black friends. At first, we just would leave right after rehearsal or a game. We didn't want to horse around with the white fellows too much, because we didn't want things to go too far. One afternoon while we were still in the locker room, a couple of white dudes came over and started asking us a lot of questions, like: 'How come we didn't have much to say and why did we always leave early. . . , ' things like that. And we laid it out for them. We told them what it was like being in a school where we were the minority. They said they thought we

didn't like them and looked mad all the time; and that
they couldn't figure out what was wrong.

After that, we found out that the other guys had some
problems too, not racial, but different kinds of problems.
Now there are seven of us (three black, four white) that go
around together all the time and even our parent's know
each other now and visit each other a lot. I found that it's
really not true that you can't have white friends without
losing your black identity.

Friendships are usually based on mutual likes and dislikes, and
the security of being able to have an argument and know the
friendship will still remain intact. It is true that black and white
friendships are not particularly encouraged by the society in which
we live. There are all kinds of barriers: separate neighborhoods,
churches, clubs, not dancing at the same public ballrooms or
socials, and not attending the same schools, except usually after
much controversy. Blacks and whites are sometimes reluctant to
begin friendships deeper than passing acquaintances for fear of
being ridiculed by their family or friends or maybe losing some
allegiance to their black or white identity. In spite of all that, black
and white friendships can and do grow, but sometimes very
delicately and more slowly than between those of the same racial or
ethnic background.

In some integrated nursery and elementary schools, black and
white pupils get along pretty much on an individual basis.
Sometimes they become close friends, visiting back and forth, and
attending birthday and other parties given for each other. They go
on picnics, museum jaunts, and other places together, sometimes
accompanied by the parents of either or both races. The friendships
are fun and undemanding as far as the racial aspect is concerned.
In short, the parents discourage any such talk about "differences"
in race, and appear to be happy that their children are enjoying
themselves.

However, once in high school, black students report noticeable
changes in these friendships on the part of the white students and
eventually begin reacting to these changes. Here is what a black
high school student who had attended integrated schools from
elementary to high school had to say:

I went to an integrated school all my life where most of the kids were white. I had a lot of friends, that is, until we got into high school. The first thing a black student notices is that while the black friends still act the same, the white ones are beginning to act 'funny.' In the hall their conversations get briefer and briefer. They stop talking when you join them. If you invite them over like usual, they have something else to do. You may hear them talking about a great party they either gave or went to and you realize that not only did they not invite you like usual, but they didn't even *tell* you about it. Being black, you know it will look odd if you question them about it, because it will look as if you're a 'tom,' and feel bad because 'whitey' don't seem to want you around. But the truth is, you didn't think of them as 'whitey' but as friends. You wonder and worry about what you must have done to make them mad. At the same time you wonder and worry that the other black kids have noticed what's going on. You just never think they may be going through the same things you are. If you do get the courage to ask what's wrong, the whites just deny everything and ask *you* what's wrong and keep on acting the way they did before you asked. Finally, either you or another black kid brings up the 'white problem.' When you compare notes, you find that the thing happening to you is happening to most of your black friends in this integrated school, too. Then you begin to meet the new black kids, who've never been in an integrated school before. Most of them don't trust the white kids in the first place. When they hear from us what has been happening, they always ask, 'What did you expect?' Then we, the blacks, start sitting together at lunch and since the white kids don't bother to sit with us, it's finally known throughout the school as the 'Black Table.' It could have been the 'Mixed Table,' but the white students either won't sit with us, or if one or two try to, the white or new black students give them a hassle. After the 'Black Table' and our talks, the blacks usually ask for black students organization, exclusively black. We want to get our heads together and find out who we are and at the same time we want the white kids to know we understand that they don't want to socialize with us and to know that we do very well without them being around us, too. But then they always get mad and ask what did they do or how come when they're nice to us, we're mean to them.

## Cooperation

On the other hand, black and white students sometimes do get together and try to deal with the problems of racial friction. In one integrated high school, where the population of black students, though still a minority, had grown, a group of students, black and white, organized a human relations club. They felt that such an organization would help head off or solve racial conflicts by giving the students a place to meet and discuss problems, with a view toward solving them together.

They needed an advisor or sponsor and out of all the black and white teachers, only one teacher who was white and female consented to help. The students then enthusiastically began recruiting members. A couple of past-members had this to say:

> We found in recruiting that some of the toughest, meanest looking whites or blacks were really for integration, but they just didn't think that it would work in that school or that neighborhood. Some said they wouldn't join yet, but would help to protect both the black and white students who wanted to try. After the membership drives, we set up forums and invited guest speakers. We found that even the kids who weren't yet members showed up. They found that black and white kids could have really fierce arguments on points of racism and still not break up the club, and a lot of them began to join. But after we graduated, the club didn't get much support from the school administration and finally there were no more members.

The students in this high school recognized the racial problems and tried to solve them by going directly to the students. The school

*Black and white elementary school children skip rope together on the playground at a Florida school after school officials made desegration policies work.* (Wide World Photo)

itself should have taken a positive view of the students' efforts and adopted the human relations club. Perhaps the racial conflicts could have been lessened if the students had seen the school expand its club's efforts in fostering better understanding between the students of both races.

## Black Pride

Not so long ago, about the worst thing a person could be called was "Black." Everything black was bad: black lies, black clouds, black hearts, black-balled, black-magic, and black-face. Everything white was good: white lies, white clouds, white-magic, and white-face. White is spoken of as pure. Black is that which is sinister. Even white sugar is thought of as "refined."

If black people had a preference as to what they wished to be called it could have been Negro, colored, or brown. Those who preferred "Negro" felt there was much more dignity in the name, than "colored" which, to them, sounded apologetic, or "brown" which was not always individually accurate. Also it was felt that since "Negro" meant "black" anyway, it was more to the truth, but was a nicer way of saying it.

Others felt that "Negro" was too harsh sounding and felt that "colored" or "brown" grated on the nerves less. Then along came young black people with their "Black Pride" slogans, taking the sting out of "Negro" or "colored" or even "black" by declaring that the people were simply and beautifully "black." No more could a person be hurt by being called "black." Even the really derogatory term "nigger" became less bothersome in the flurry of *open* black search for identity and respectful recognition.

Black people have always had a sense of pride, but others have declined to believe there was such a thing. When "black pride" was accidentally found by whites, it was considered "uppity" and dealt with as harshly as circumstances would allow. Blacks had the added difficulty of searching out their identity. This has been due to confused trails to past and present accomplishments of blacks both within and beyond our country. Much of this search has been unknown to many whites. If they thought of it at all, it seemed relatively unimportant in the scheme of things. Whites were somewhat astonished to discover that not only did blacks themselves wish to search and learn of black accomplishments, but they wanted whites to also do so. And whites strongly resisted the addition to the curriculum of Black History, Afro-American History, Black Arts and Crafts, and/or the accreditation of them.

Still, blacks like others, are individuals, and are not agreed on all things. Some still prefer to be called "Negro," "colored," or "brown" and must be respected for this. If they express a particular desire, then oblige, but white people cannot go far wrong in using the term "Black" in connection with black people. Not only because the majority of blacks have accepted this appellation, but because there no longer is the bleak hostility attached to "Black" as there once was.

## Student Demands

In an integrated school, black students will sometimes notice there are some discrepancies in the facilities as regards the black contingent of the school. Some demands, growing out of frustration and anger, can sometimes be regarded as a kind of "nit-picking." However, some demands are really legitimate and obvious.

Here is a partial list of demands that some black high school students presented to their principal, which began with these words:

> Due to a lack of Black teachers, Black history and only a few Black students, the white community of this school is ignorant of the intelligence, and awareness of the Black community and the slights they are subjected to.
> Lack of 'open' plays — black students who aspire to appear in the school plays are told that they cannot be cast if the characters are a white family, as in "Death of a Salesman." We feel that a student should not be judged on his color, but on his acting ability:
> We demand that white students have the chance to select "soul food" or not in the cafeteria, just as black students experience the same privilege as regards "white" foods in the same cafeteria.

We demand that Black History should be in the curriculum with full credit, so that white teachers get a chance to realize that there has been a missing part of American History.

The list of demands ends with a quote from author James Baldwin:

It is necessary while in darkness, to know that there is a light somewhere to know that in oneself, waiting to be found, there is a light.

## Changing Patterns

The question, "How can a white student talk openly with a black without sounding prejudiced or hurting their feelings?" illustrates the fact that white and black students do not always look at one another simply as other human beings who are just as vulnerable as themselves in certain situations. Getting to know a person calls for some skill and tact. Blundering in, asking some wild question, making an unthinking remark, statement or judgement without building a good base of understanding, could be courting disaster.

Here is an example of just such a disaster. Two female freshmen, one black the other white, attending an eastern college, had roomed together for about a week and seemed to have arrived at an agreeable relationship. One evening the black girl was stretched across her bed reading while the white girl sat before the mirror applying make-up before her date picked her up. Suddenly, in disgust, she threw down her eye shadow brush and said, according to her black roommate: "Boy! I wish I were like you!" When the black roommate inquired as to what she meant, she was told, "Then I wouldn't have to worry about how I put on make-up, nobody could see it anyway." The black girl yelled, "What!" and leaped from the bed grabbing up the white girl's make-up and began to furiously apply it all over her face, while yelling at her frightened roommate, "Can you see it, can you see it now?"

The really odd thing is that the black girl was as fair as the white girl, but because of the myth of color, and the ideas of the "differences" between black and white, the white student unconsciously rejected what her eyes told her. In reaching for safe ground on which to base their very new relationship, she voiced something she had either heard before or by deductive reasoning figured that if black people are black, then color cannot show up on them. Whether conscious or not, she succeeded in helping to break the tenuous thread of a chance to find out once and for all if there was really that much of a difference between herself and the black girl.

The black roommate, on the other hand, had probably been more than a little wary of a white "friendship" and the moment she heard something that "proved" how insensitive some white people can be, reacted in an overly dramatic way. The action and the reaction ruined any chance for a friendship to grow. The black student reported that she requested to move in with a black roommate soon after the incident.

Sometimes a white student will appear over-eager to participate in friendships with black students and thus becomes suspect. The black kids might feel he is insincere, that he wants to become friends because his fellow whites reject him for some reason or other, or that he might just be "putting them on" in order to eventually "put them down" at a crucial moment. In short, the black kids, just as the white kids, sometimes simply distrust exaggerated overtures to befriend them, especially across the color line.

A young college student, white and female, reports:

> I tried very hard to make friends with the black girls in my dormitory. I never had the opportunity of knowing black kids and I was anxious to meet them and hoped that they would accept my friendship. But I found that when I would speak, they wouldn't; when I would smile, they would frown; and when on occasion, through nervousness, didn't speak they would aggressively do so.
> One day, I pushed open the door of the washroom and accidentally struck a black girl standing there. While I was apologizing, she was calling me names and pushing me while the other black girls laughed. I finally ran from the room crying. I decided that it was impossible to make friends with black bigots and I was through trying.

About an hour later, the same girls with whom I had had trouble in the washroom, knocked on my open door and came in, including the girl who had called me names and pushed me. Before they could say a word I really let them have it! I told them I didn't need their friendship, that I didn't care what they said or did to me, I hated them all. One of them quietly handed me a tissue, and when I stopped yelling and crying, they began telling me that they were sorry for what had happened, but that they had received the same kind of treatment from some of the teachers, counselors and students on and off campus. They admitted that they had begun to think that all of us were alike, that it was sometimes hard to tell the enemy from the friends when the enemies were all the same color. We began laughing. When some of my white friends standing in the hall joined us, we called out for a pizza. We believe our domitory is about the only one on campus that has integrated friendships.

When asked if she thought the friendships she found there would carry on after she has graduated, she said:

No, I don't think so. We will probably write a little to each other, then stop, because that's what usually happens to most out-of-state friendships. But it's mostly what our society thinks about color that will probably end it.

After a good friendship has been established, most of the questions the black or white student wanted to ask have all been answered without actually having to voice questions at all. In fact, the white student who has become friends with a black student will resent even more than the black certain questions posed by other whites who are either acquaintances or strangers.

Being in school with black students, as far as some adults feel, is practically the same as working at the same job with them. After being with blacks all day, when the end of the workday or school day arrives, they part company not to see or hear from each other until the next school or workday. Sadly, black and white people lose the opportunity to become close enough to one another to understand what the other is going through in everyday life. This is the way segregation works. It has been very effective for a long time. However, the pattern seems to be changing. Even though we have been conditioned to believe that every black-white meeting will be explosive and harmful and that we must be kept apart, we seem to be drawing closer and closer together. This has come about largely because students seem to want to know for themselves rather than be told.

"Hunky" is a derogatory term once used to describe Hungarian immigrants who came to America. Blacks took "hunky" and turned it into "honky" using it to describe any white person who hates or hurts black people. Blacks use the term the same way whites use "nigger." However, blacks do not think of all white students, teachers, or other adults as "honkies."

Black and white students who wish to help make life better between the races should get together and seriously consider a working human relations organization within the school. It should also be open to the help of the teachers and the school administration. Within this organization, polls of the students' views should be taken and discussed along with their complaints and suggestions. The student body should have access to such information and student action should be taken to help make things more favorable for interracial interaction without conflict.

# ELEVEN

# PROBLEMS OF PRINCIPALS

*There is a modern force . . . pushing leaders everywhere
to reflect on what are right things to do. This is the force
of self-determination now alive in the world: the idea that
all people, from families to work groups to nations and
communities of nations can have every right to exercise
their ability to choose some considerable measure of
conscious self-influence over their destinies. The
Administrator's Job: Issues and Dilemmas, by R.K. Ready*

Principals who are confronted with the fact of having both blacks
and whites in their schools may have a number of questions on their
minds. Some principals, for instance, have broached the following
kinds of questions: What can be said to parents, upset over
desegregation, to help them accept interracial education? Are
human relations classes necessary for teachers, all other personnel,
and the principal? Should black students be given special
privileges, such as their own exclusive clubs, etc? Should the
schools include a human relations officer or staff? Should parents
be asked to act as volunteer hall guards, instead of policemen to
protect students from inside or outside agitators?

In these times, principals of our elementary and high schools
sometimes find themselves in the role of arbitrator or referee when
previously all-white or all-black schools come under the spotlight of
impending or actual integration. This is especially so when the
school in question is surrounded by either all-white or all-black
neighborhoods, where integration by busing is required.

Principals are understandably concerned with the problems of
peacefully integrating a school. They naturally wish to maintain
peace so that an atmosphere conducive to learning can be
experienced by all the school's students. Everyone functions better
under productive orderliness, including the teachers, and this
makes for a better prepared graduating student.

As is expected in any school, the principal should be concerned with implementing plans which ensure that all students receive proper attention from the teachers. The principal must make it clear from the outset that students understand that harming one another will be met with swift and decisive action — especially if found to be based on racial disharmony. The principal must also inform parents, teachers, and students that they are expected to work together in the best interests of the school.

To accomplish these aims, the principal first needs to understand his own feelings in the matter. Does he feel equal to the undertaking? Does he feel a desire to implement the kinds of guidelines that can make integration a positive and effective program in his school? In his view is there merit in the schools' role in integration, whether it is by busing or open housing? Can he put forth his full energies toward guiding his school firmly through a program designed to phase out the destructive elements of racial animosity in his school?

In addition, the principal should assess the varying kinds of pressures which may be exerted on him through the feelings of his own family, friends, and neighbors regarding a positive program of integration in his school. If these important people in his private life reveal negative attitudes, will he be able to cope, remaining unhampered in his inventiveness and effectiveness in seeing that the transistion in his school is a positive, smooth experience for his students?

A principal should make clear to all concerned that it is his professional duty, responsibility and intention to work within the structure of the law and school policy as effectively and efficiently as possible.

The principal should know the feelings of the teachers, teacher-aids, counselors, social workers, school nurse, office staff, and all other auxillary staff in regard to integration insofar as the school is concerned. He needs to know what their expectations are in regard to school integration and what they are prepared to do toward making the transition a smooth and productive process.

It is, however, only fair to point out that there is the possibility that even a principal with good will and determination can run into explosive situations where disruptions result in utter chaos. Parents can infect their children with their own prejudices by giving them such ideas as it does not matter what they do to another, as long as the other person is not of the same race, color or creed. Moreover, there may be walk-outs, sit-in's, ugly chants, and worse. But, the principal who is able under such duress to still maintain his good will toward all the people and at the same time assert his positive thoughts, principles, and plans regarding desegregation, who openly maintains integration can and will work, will find sooner or later that he gains a respect albeit a grudging one from most or all of the people.

No one can say that integration is easy and that the principal's role in such a plan will be easy. Yet, most people can see that segregation as it has been known is now on its way out. There is no place in the long narrow twisting road we have taken to turn around and go back to the "good ole days" of Jim Crow.

## A Changing School Situation

Following is an example of a school which was undergoing the integration process. It demonstrates what can happen when a school is unable to maintain a continuing awareness and a growing understanding by the principal and teachers regarding the desires and needs of black and white parents and students in a school.

A few black families moved into a previously all-white neighborhood where their children entered the neighborhood elementary school quietly and without fanfare. After a time, the black parents and the white parents began to see that the students were getting along and that the students' scholastic averages were not going down.

A year or so went by during which time more and more black students began attending the school. Black parents began noticing that there was less emphasis on their children's study habits than had been true previously. There was less homework and fewer classroom assignments than before. The parents found it difficult to discuss these puzzling events with the teachers or principal. Soon some of the white parents began informing some of the black parents that if the school did not revert to its previous high standards, they would be moving in order to enroll their children in school which did maintain high standards.

PERSPECTIVES ON EDUCATION AND LEARNING

Upon asking shop teachers why certain worn out equipment was not being replaced and adequate materials provided as had been true previously when the school had been predominantly white, parents were turned away without satisfactory answers. Parents found that teachers seemed to require less and less from the students as black enrollment increased.

The black parents, now in the majority, finally made contact with the white principal. They encountered hostility as illustrated by such statements as, "If you don't like the way things are going for your 'student,' why don't you take him out?" . . . "I'm running this school; I'll make the decisions as to whether or not my teachers are doing a good job or not!" . . . "You won't come in here and run *my* school!" . . . "We didn't have any trouble here before your people came!" . . . "You're a bunch of trouble makers and I don't have to listen to you!"

It was clear that the principal was frustrated, angry and defensive. He had not been as prepared for integration as is necessary to help make it work. He had felt alone in his dilemma and tried to proceed as if the school could outwardly ignore the phenomenon of racial integration in this country and survive.

The parents, after talking things over among themselves, decided that talking with the principal was useless. They felt he did not have a clear understanding of where he stood on integration and the education of all the students, white as well as black. They formed a parent school council announcing formally to the principal that the purpose would be voluntarily perform tasks that would be of aid to the teachers and administrative staff by assuring them of more teaching time with the students. The parents believed that by taking certain extra-curricular pressures off the teachers and by demonstrating to the principal their positive interest in the students' academic development, there was a good chance that their children would then receive the kind of educational teacher involvement that had been true when the school was a predominantly white one.

The parents, however, upon perceiving that the principal still maintained a hostile silence and refused to meet with the Council, decided to work toward his removal as principal of the school. They wished to replace him with someone with a better understanding and sensitivity of the problems facing the students and community;

*Parents boycotting their children's school in a demand for the removal of the school
principal whom the parents considered "racist."* (Chicago Daily News Photo)

coupled with the knowledge and dedication needed to restore the school's past record of scholastic achievement. The Parent's School Council decided to concern itself only with the ability and dedication of the candidate, not the skin color. It happened that the candidate finally selected and acceptable to the Council was female and white.

The new principal stated that the parents in the community were far-seeing, discerning, and fair. She made it clear that she welcomed their suggestions, comments, and help. The council in return welcomed volunteer help from the parents of the students, as well as from those adults with no students in the school. Some of the outlined tasks were hall, lunchroom, and washroom duties. There were volunteers for chaperones, club advisors, and classroom aides. Both the new principal and the Council believe that the school should be the focal point of any neighborhood, "because what happens in the school is felt in just about every home or business in the area."

## Staff Development

It is fairly safe to assume that at this point in time many white teachers have not had the benefit of race relations courses. Moreover, most white teachers have had little or no personal contact with blacks in their colleges or universities or in their training programs. As a consequence, it is little wonder that they will come to an integrated classroom with less than a secure feeling, or the ability to cope with such a situation. In view of this, one white principal stated that *all* school personnel, even those who have had interracial experiences, should be required to attend a weekly race relations in-service session in order to share or clear up certain points of view.

It would seem advisable that race relations seminars be provided for all school personnel within the school setting. Such a school-sanctioned setting offers the security of soberly pursuing knowledge in a conducive atmosphere. Since race relations are a part of human relations, faculty who may have had few or no black students in the classroom, or who have had contact with few or no black teachers or staff, will certainly benefit from such an experience. Race relations seminars open the door to less conflict through better and clearer understanding. Communication between blacks and whites make this possible.

It is very important that office personnel be included in such courses. On many occasions black students, parents and visitors have remarked on the coolness or rudeness displayed to them by office personnel — both white and black. Such behavior can create tension, anxieties and anger, along with the desire to retaliate against the school in some manner.

In order to implement such in-service sessions, it might be well that a Human Relations Coordinator be appointed or hired, whose duty it is to plan sessions for the staff and give seminars. Since there probably will be varying degrees of acceptance or even none to such in-service sessions; based on ignorance and fear coupled with some amount of prejudice, the Coordinator at the first meeting should apprise the entire staff of what the sessions are intended to do. The goals of the organization or the school should be pointed out. What is expected of all personnel should be fully explained. Finally, assurances must be given that the views and experiences of those in attendance will be heard and respected, that all questions will be answered. The Coordinator cannot be viewed as an all-knowing expert, but rather must be viewed as dedicated to the path of searching for truth in our race relations.

## Separatism

Giving students special privileges based on color though not desirable is understandable from the point of view of black students. They do not need "special privileges," if they are included, in the full sense of the word, in the school's social as well as academic activities. All students should have the same privileges and should be held equally accountable for their actions when they run counter to these privileges. Students seeking security by excluding others from their social activities on campus are merely reacting against what they see as discrimination. It, therefore, is up to the school principal to point this out to them in a positive fashion and to actively seek more suitable outlets for the students than separatism.

If a principal is suddenly confronted by black or white students asking for separate club rooms, restricted as to the color of the students participating in club (black or white), the students must be made aware of the law forbidding segregation based on race, color, creed, or national origin. If, for example, students wish a Black History Club or a Black Students Alliance on campus, then, according to desegregation laws, the membership must be open to *all* students on campus, with the possible exception of age or school year. Students must understand that segregation may not be practiced in the school with its sanction. The adding of black history or culture to the school curriculum or certain foods to the cafeteria menu is acceptable, because it enhances the school. Further, it may help broaden racial understanding by other students. As far as theatre within the school is concerned, no student may be refused a part that he can play because his color may not be the same as was anticipated by the author. In short, the principal who accepts color as part of an individual, and not as a restriction, will favorably influence the teachers and students in his school.

A principal needs to be especially sensitive to the kinds of influence affecting both black and white students in a newly integrated school. Everything in a previously segregated school is already established, set-up, begun without any thought of the newly integrated students. The old ways must be reconsidered. Measures must be taken to ensure that there is an open climate that will allow new students to grow, to stretch out and become an integral part of the whole, without reference to color or any other extraneous criteria.

It probably is not possible for a principal to change racial attitudes of all teachers, other personnel, or students. A principal probably can, however, create the kind of climate in which all students may equally participate. This can best be accomplished through expressing his attitudes to the students and in his openness toward faculty and other personnel in advocating a "no-nonsense" policy of desegregation.

### Student Harassment

In some integrated school situations, principals and staff will be confronted with the fact that some black students engage in bullying and harassing behavior toward white students, and exhibit disrespect for teachers. One white student, a junior attending a high school in a Northern school district, writes that black students "either stand or sit around in the halls poking fun at 'whitey'. When they *do* show up in class, they are either late or so discourteous to the teacher — white or black — it makes me sick." The student goes on to say "The whites are afraid of the blacks, and the blacks don't give a damn about anyone. They gather in droves and seem to *live* on the fear in 'whitey's face." This student also relates "I'm afraid to do any extracurricular activity, to stay after school at all, or to even be at school early for fear of the blacks."

One wonders whether this student has had a chance to become friends with any blacks, and if not, why not. The student does point out that many of the black students go to class and behave like "beautiful human beings." But the student seems to feel they are the minority and there is no indication from the student of any friendships with blacks. This is sad.

In part, the type of behavior described reflects segregated living patterns and distrust which continue to exist in certain communities. In part, the behavior may reflect confusion and insecurity on the part of the black students in the adolescent search for identity.

Whatever the case, it is a problem that is necessary to confront and to remedy. It is the kind of situation which calls for engagement and not a "hands off" or "I'll take care of that, if it ever happens again" policy. The problem needs to be brought out into the open. It must be discussed frankly among teachers and administrative staff. Sessions need to be held with black and white students together to discuss the matter and seek solutions. It must be emphasized to the students that racist behavior in the schools cannot be tolerated. Problems do not simply go away — and may well get worse — by ignoring them or keeping them under wraps in the offices of the school administrators.

TWELVE

# WHERE DO WE GO FROM HERE?

*. . . the conditions of the society make it imperative that the schools assume a role of creative reconstruction. Inquiry in Social Studies,* Byron G. Massialas and Benjamin C. Cox.

To teach in any school, anywhere, anyplace, a teacher cannot allow himself (or herself) to become wrapped in a web that will keep him out of touch with reality. It is much easier to believe (when certain groups of people are different than the ethnic, racial, or nationality one is part of, and most used to) that the stereotypes one hears of others are probably more true than is true for one's own group. These "myths" may allow an individual to feel safe and superior for a while, but informed people soon find out how false and unsatisfying they are, and begin to realize that the country's future really rests on the fate of all of our young.

The breaking down of the walls of prejudice and hatred requires a thorough process of reeducation. People are going to have to educate each other through questions, answers and dialogue. It is not merely a question of white leaders conferring with black leaders. That is done all of the time, and it really is not enough by itself. Solutions require that black and white teachers teaching in schools together know each other socially as well as professionally. The white housewife and the black housewife living next door to each other need to go beyond merely nodding at each other as they happen to pass one another. Whites and blacks working together need to really talk to each other. Black and white classmates need to begin talking and listening to each other rather than ignoring each other except for fighting. Everyone of us has the power to help make things right between all Americans, and perhaps with the rest of the world as well.

Responsibility has always been placed on the younger generation to solve the world's problems. Sometimes the new generation solves many of the previous generations unsolved or unresolved problems. But insofar as racial quandaries are concerned, they have been remanded over and over to the *next* younger generation. Thus the most obvious problem still facing us today is that of racism. The most neglected effort is that of educating ourselves to one another. And, in the case of many a black person, he lacks knowledge of even himself. Since his introduction to this country, his history has been systematically shrouded in mystery and half-truths. His ancient past was, in part, glorious, but upon arrival in America, this past became cloaked in obscurity, while his presence here was treated in the same killing manner.

## Futility of Racism

Racism is a dead-end street, leading only to frustration, fear, hatred of others, and finally to a chilling, dehumanizing self-hatred. Because of racism and all of its ugly ramifications, many black children, as well as adults, have suffered great damage to their self-esteem. Our school system, our churches, our synagogues, magazines, newspapers, textbooks, radio, television have frequently either ignored or ridiculed the ancestral greatness of the peoples of Africa. Africa, the birthplace of mankind, has long been laughingly called "the dark continent" instead of being heralded as the "Mother Nation" of us all, a common heritage and brotherhood that all men share . . . whether they believe it or not.

Now that information on the history of blacks, the lives of blacks, the beauty of blacks, the contributions of blacks is pouring forth, we are finding increased questioning and "soul-searching" among whites. More and more white people are becoming aware of and appalled by the damage racial prejudice has done to individuals and to society as a whole. At the same time, we have been experiencing a kind of pulling apart of blacks and whites within our high schools, colleges, and universities, students and teachers alike. We are finding that though blacks need black education, whites need it even more. Self-esteem is a must for sheer survival. When others esteem us, we find that hostilities and misunderstandings are lessened.

White students complain that they are rejected by black students whenever they attempt to join, help, or befriend them. They invariably say, "I understand though, they (the blacks) have to do their own thing in order to find pride in themselves. And we really don't have too much in common because their culture is different — they talk differently than we do, eat different foods. Anyway, I've decided to do something else, so it's just as well." And through all of this rhetoric one very real feeling comes through, relief. When these students are asked what is black culture, they try to cover ignorance for a brief while, then finally say they really don't know. When they are asked what is white culture, and to please show the difference between black and white culture, they are again at a loss. They then usually state they they do not know what blacks really want.

Most blacks want only what America promises its citizens: The chance to exploit their talents, in the field of their own choosing; the individual right to live where they choose; to experience the same treatment in any court of the land (under the law) as other citizens; the right to belong to any union, craft, trade or profession; the right to even fail without the stigma of, "Well, what else could you expect, he's black you know!" Blacks want the same mobility and opportunities as any white citizen — nothing more, nothing less.

In order to overcome distrust and animosity, whites will have to understand what stereotypes are meant to achieve, and why. Whites will have to come to understand what they really feel, as well as why. There must come a time when whites can accept the fact that they are the ones who have to fight racial prejudices even harder than their black brothers. And they must be able to fight a good fight without crippling guilt feelings.

Natural teachers (non-school teachers as well as school teachers, inside as well as outside the homes) have the serious charge of educating the young to a world which they never made. In order to make this a better world for our children, racial prejudice has to be shown for what it really is, *a stupid waste of time.*

Why, one wonders, is it necessary for the people of our country, from various backgrounds and cultures, to continue to suffer the emotional and moral distortions wrought by the web of racism? Why, for instance the following?:

I am Japanese, 16 and a high school student. There are some black students I like very much, but I'm afraid that if I am too friendly, asking them to my house, going to parties with them, that my white friends will drop by friendship. I don't have many white friends, and only a few Japanese friends (there aren't many here). My mother is what I would call liberal; but my father says he hates blacks and whites, and that I should limit my friendships to Japanese, or maybe even Chinese.

I am Jewish, and a high school teacher. Blacks seem to think they are the only ones with trouble. I notice that whenever I walk up to a group of Gentiles, teachers or otherwise, they either stop talking or walk away. In a recent meeting of some of the administrators and faculty, I had the distinct feeling that had I not been there, certain topics would have been discussed. I can understand racial distrust and, if you will, dislike of the blacks, but Jews have brought a distinct cultural heritage to this country, such as no other ethnic or racial group has. I don't understand it.

I am white and employed as a company representative. I visit colleges and universities to find graduate students who qualify as candidates for certain positions with the company. While I have no trouble interviewing white applicants, I find that it is difficult for me to interview black applicants with the same degree of smoothness. I do not believe that I am prejudiced, but since I understand that black people have different life-styles than whites, I constantly worry that the same questions that we ask the white candidates, might offend the black candidates. In my position with the company, I must also weigh whether or not the candidates will fit comfortably into the whole atmosphere of the company, and when I am looking into a black face, rather than a white one, to me, it's a whole new ballgame. I wonder with whom he will associate, not only in the company, but after working hours as well . . . and where will he live. The company is not in the inner city . . .

Then I discover that I am either smiling too much, or not at all; my hands become wet with perspiration; I find myself wondering if the candidate notices all this; and then I find myself generally becoming hostile before the interview is over, even though this is wrong. I realize that something is wrong, but I know that I am *not* prejudiced. I wonder how can I deal with the whole thing. I believe that I must find a new job.

I am Jewish and white. When I was in high school I knew that I was liberal and harbored no "racist" feelings toward the blacks who attended the same high school as myself. In fact, I congratulated myself on the fact that I never even thought of racial "differences". But one day something happened that I will never forget and finally woke me up. I got into an argument with a fellow student over some literary point or other and in the heat of the argument only barely stopped myself from saying to him, "Don't you argue with me, don't you see that I'm *White?*" I still shudder whenever I think of it.

I am white and a teacher in a small town in the South. I had an occasion to visit a northern city one year and after attending a meeting had the opportunity of meeting the speaker who was black. She in turn invited me to dinner with her family and friends. I found that her husband was white and their friends that evening at dinner were black, white and Oriental. I confessed to them that evening that I had never been in the company of people other than white, and especially not in the company of an interracially married couple.
The whole evening with these people was exciting for me. We talked of many things, race being only one of the topics. The evening flew by. I never talk at home, or at least have little to say, but in these peoples' company there was freedom to speak of whatever I chose without fear of anger or ridicule by the listeners. I will never forget it. Two nights later they invited me to join them for dinner in a neighborhood restaurant. In the town in which I live,

this restaurant would be open to only those with a lot of money. Our town is a very poor one. At first I was overwhelmed by the place, to the extent that I forgot my hostess was black. When others came past our table and began speaking to her and her husband, I suddenly realized who I was . . . and who they were, and also simultaneously, the hell that could await me at home if anyone there found out. They invited me to their home for a talk and drinks afterward, and I went. They had a large home and invited me to be their guest for the night because of the lateness of the hour. They promised to take me back to my hotel after breakfast. I accepted. This was a new world to me. But, later on, I became nervous and when the house was dark and everyone asleep, I quietly left for my hotel. If anyone found out at home, I might have been able to explain visiting in the home of an integrated couple, but explaining why I slept there would have been impossible.

They called my hotel the next day in great concern, and I explained to them that they were the nicest people I had ever met and I had had the greatest time, but that it wasn't possible to ever visit with them again or even to acknowledge that I had ever met them. They seemed to understand. I'll never forget them.

## Re-education

These examples represent tragic episodes in the lives of people who otherwise would have been unfettered by racial bonds. Tradition, habit, sanctioned by positive law, or allowed to exist in the absence of positive law, caused persons such as these to feel themselves prevented from acting as free individuals as far as race relations were concerned. It is understandably difficult for people to fly in the face of tradition and habit. But today, now, the law of our land has unfettered us from the bonds of blind acquiescence to outmoded habits and traditions. We are, now, free to associate, communicate and to educate each other. There would seem to be no better place to begin than in our educational systems — from kindergarten through graduate school.

People are never too old or too young to learn or to be their natural human selves as can be exemplified by the picture at the end of this chapter and the following two quotations from papers written by graduate students after completing a race relations course:

> What I wish is that there would be many more white students involved in this type of dialogue, because few have had any direct confrontation with blacks to hear and listen to what it is to be black. This 'white ignorance' of blacks is verbalized so often in such phrases as, 'Gee, I didn't know that' or 'That's no different than what white people do or think.'

> I guess this learning must be thoroughly developed in the schools from elementary to college with Black History or Black Culture courses . . . The learning must be done by the children and young adults who are in the schools where the information is. Then they must disseminate their information among their parents and friends. Changes that are to come will come through the young adults of today be they black or white.

> We need so much to get to know one another . . . I have learned that courage, flexibility, openess, open-mindedness, and love are the best characteristics one can have in his interactions with others. Coupled with knowledge and creativity, these attributes give a teaching candidate exceptional chances in the inner city school.

> There are no pat answers, I know . . . I will probably solve very few problems in the society in which we live; but any insights I have to recognize short-comings and any gumption that I have to stand up to the wrongs and the injustices will surely have been nourished by a class such as this.

An instant friendship was formed between Robin Brosset (left) and Paula Moye upon Robin's arrival at Bagley school, September 8, 1971. Robin was bused from home to the school as part of Pontiac, Michigan's attempt to create racial balance, as ordered by the courts. Even though parents were protesting the busing order, the children involved seemed to take the situation in stride.

(UPI Photo)

BIBLIOGRAPHY

# BIBLIOGRAPHY

Adoff, Arnold, ed., *I Am the Darker Brother: An Anthology of Modern Poems by Negro Americans*, Macmillan, N.Y., 1968.

Alland, Alexander Jr., *Evolution and Human Behavior*, The Natural History Press, Garden City, N.Y., 1967.

Allport, Gordon W., *The Nature of Prejudice*, Doubleday Anchor, N.Y., 1958.

Anderson, Lester W. and Van Dyke, Lauren A., *Secondary School Administration*, 2nd Edition, Houghton-Mifflin, 1972.

Aptheker, Herbert, *Negro Slave Revolts in the United States*, International Publishers, N.Y., 1939.

Baldwin, James, *Nobody Knows My Name*, Dell, N.Y., 1963.

Baldwin, James, *The Fire Next Time*, Dell, N.Y., 1963.

Beck, John M. and Saxe, Richard W., *Teaching the Culturally Disadvantaged Pupil*, Charles C. Thomas Publisher, Springfield, Illinois, 1965.

Bennett, Lerone, *Before the Mayflower*, Johnson Publishing Co., Chicago, 1962.

Bennett, Lerone, Jr., *The Challenge of Blackness*, Johnson Publishing Co., Chicago, 1972.

Billingsley, Andrew, *Black Families in White America*, Prentice-Hall, New Jersey, 1968.

Bontemps, Arna and Conroy, Jack, *Anyplace But Here*, Hill and Wang, N.Y., 1966.

Brooks, Gwendolyn, *The Bean Eaters*, Harper & Bros., N.Y., 1960.

Browder, Lesley H., Jr., *Emerging Patterns of Administrative Accountability*, Cutcheon Publishing Corp., Berkeley, Calif., 1971.

Brown, Claude, *Manchild in the Promised Land*, Signet, N.Y., 1965.

Butcher, Margaret Just, *The Negro in American Culture*, Mentor, N.Y., 1956.

Chestang, Leon, "The Dilemma of Biracial Adoption," *Social Work*, May 1972. (Available in reprint).

Chestang, Leon, *Character Development in a Hostile Environment*, University of Chicago School of Social Service Administration, November 1972.

Chestang, Leon, "The Issue of Race in Casework Practice," *The Social Welfare Forum*, 1970. (Available in reprint).

*Chicago Sun-Times*, "How city pupils fared, grade school by grade school," June 17, 1971.

Clark, Kenneth B., *Prejudice and Your Child*, 2nd Edition, Beacon Press, Boston, 1968.

Clark, Vincent E., *Unmarried Mothers*, The Free Press, Glencoe, Illinois, 1961.

Cleaver, Eldridge, *Soul On Ice*, McGraw-Hill, N.Y., 1968.

Cloward, Richard A. and Ohlin Lloyd E., *Delinquency and Opportunity*, The Free Press, Glencoe, Illinois, 1961.

Cohen, Morris R. and Nagel, Ernest, *An Introduction to Logic and Scientific Method*, Harcourt, Brace, N.Y., 1934.

Cohen, Robert, *The Color of Man*, Random House, N.Y., 1968.

Cooley, Charles Horton, *Human Nature and the Social Order*, Charles Scribner's Sons, N.Y., 1922.

Commager, Henry Steele, *The American Mind*, Yale University Press, New Haven, 1950.

*Daedalus*: Journal of the American Acadamy of Arts and Sciences, Color and Race, Spring 1967.

Davidson, Basil, *African Kingdoms*, Great Ages of Man, Time-Life Books, New York, 1966.

Davis, Allison, *Social-Class Influences Upon Learning*, Harvard U Press, Cambridge, Mass., 1965.

Davis, John P., "The Negro in American Sports," *The American Negro Reference Book*, ed., John P. Davis, Prentice-Hall, 1966, V.2.

Dewey, John, *Logic: The Theory of Inquiry*, N.Y., Henry Holt, 1938.

Douglas, Frederick, *Narrative of the Life of Frederick Douglass*, Signet, N.Y., 1968.

Drake, St. Clair and Cayton Horace R., *Black Metropolis*, Harcourt, Brace & Co., N.Y., 1945.

Drisko, Carol F. and Toppin, Edgar A., *The Unfinished March*, Doubleday, N.Y., 1967.

Duberman, Martin, "Black Power," *Partisan Review*, Winter 1968.

DuBois, W.E.B., *Souls of Black Folks*, Fawcett, N.Y., 1961.

Dunn, L.C. and Dobzhansky, Th., *Heredity, Race and Society*, Mentor, N.Y., 1959.

Durham, Phillip and Jones, Everett L., *The Negro Cowboys*, Cornwall Press, Cornwall, N.Y., 1965.

221

Elkins, Stanley, *Slavery: A Problem in American Institutional & Intellectual Life,* Grosset & Dunlap, N.Y., 1963.

Ellison, Ralph, *Invisible Man,* Signet Books, N.Y., 1952.

*Equality of Educational Opportunity,* U.S. Office of Education, Harold Howe II, Commissioner, Government Printing Office, Volume II, 1966.

Erikson, Erik H., *Childhood and Society,* W.W. Norton, N.Y., 1963.

Fair, Ronald L., *Many Thousand Gone,* Victor Gonllancz, London, 1965.

Ferman, Louis A., Kornbluh, Joyce L., and Haber Alan, eds., *Poverty in America,* The Univ. of Michigan Press, Ann Arbor, 1965.

Firth, Raymand, *Human Types,* The New American Library, 1958.

Franklin, John Hope and Starr, Isidore, *The Negro in the 20th Century: A Reader On The Struggle For Civil Rights,* Vintage Books, 1967.

Franklin, John Hope, "A Brief History of the Negro in the United States," *The American Negro Reference Book,* op. cit.

Franklin, John Hope, *Reconstruction,* The University of Chicago Press, Chicago, 1961.

Frazier, Franklin, *Black Bourgeoise,* Collier Books, N.Y., 1967.

Gergen, Kenneth J., "The Significance of Color in Human Relations," *Daedalus,* The Journal of the American Academy of Arts and Sciences, Spring 1967.

Glazer, Nathan and Moynihan, Daniel, *Beyond The Melting Pot,* MIT Press, Cambridge, Mass., 1963.

Grant, Joanne, *Black Protest: History, Documents and Analyses,* Fawcett, N.Y., 1968.

Groh, George W., *The Black Migration,* Waybright & Talley, N.Y., 1972.

Handlin, Oscar, *Race and Nationality In American Life,* Little, Brown & Co., N.Y., 1957.

Handlin, Oscar, *The Uprooted,* Little, Brown & Co., N.Y., 1951.

Harrington, Michael, "The Will to Abolish Poverty," *The Saturday Review,* July 27, 1968.

Harrington, Michael, *The Other American,* Macmillan, N.Y., 1962.

Havinghurst, Robert J., "Requirements for a Valid New Criticism," *Crisis in Urban Education,* eds., Lawrence A. Fink and Raymond A. Ducharme, Jr., Xerox College Publishing, Waltham, Mass. Ginn & Co., 1971.

Havinghurst, Robert J., *The Public Schools of Chicago,* The Board of Education of the City of Chicago, 1964.

Havighurst, Robert J. and Neugarten, Berniece, *Society and Education,* 3rd Edition, Allyn & Bacon, Boston, 1968.

Havighurst, Robert J., *Education in Metropolitan Areas,* Allyn and Bacon, Boston, 1971.

Hughes, Langston, *The Best of Simple,* Hill and Wang, 1961.

Hughes, Langston, *The Langston Hughes Reader,* George Braziller, Inc., N.Y., 1958.

Hundt, Reed, "New Teacher," *Crisis in Urban Education,* op cit.

Hurst, Charles G., Jr., *Passport to Freedom,* Linnett Books, Hamden, Conn., 1972.

*Images of the Negro in America*, ed. by Darwin T. Turner and Jean M. Bright, D.C. Heath, Boston, 1965.

*International Library of Negro Life and History*, Publishers Co., N.Y., 1967.

James, William, *Pragmatism*, Longmans, Green, N.Y., 1948.

James, William, *Selected Papers on Philosophy*, Everyman's Librarh, London, 1927.

James, William, *The Varieties of Religious Experience*, Modern Library, (Copywright William James, 1902).

Jones, LeRoi, "Blues, Jazz, and the Negro," *The American Negro Reference Book*, op. cit. 1966.

Jones, LeRoi, *Tales*, Grove Press, Inc., N.Y., 1967.

Kain, John F. and Persky, Joseph J., "Alternatives to the Gilded Ghetto," *Crisis in Urban Education*, op. cit.

Katz, William Loren, *A Teachers' Guide to American Negro History*, Quadrangle Books, Chicago, 1968.

Kozol, Jonathan, *Death at an Early Age*, Bantam, N.Y., 1967.

Lewis, Anthony and The New York Times, *Portrait of a Decade*, Bantam, N.Y., 1965.

Lewis, Oscar, *La Vida*, Vintage, N.Y., 1965.

Lincoln, C. Eric, "The American Protest Movement for Negro Rights," *The American Negro Reference Book*, op. cit.

Lincoln, C. Eric, "Color and Group Identity in the United States," *Daedalus*, Spring, 1967. op. cit.

Lomax, Louis E., *The Negro Revolt*, Signet, 1963.

Meltzer, Milton and Meier, August, *Time of Trial, Time of Hope*, Doubleday, N.Y., 1966.

Merton, Robert K., *Social Theory and Social Structure*, "The Self-Fulfilling Prophecy", The Free Press, Glencoe, Illinois, 1949.

Malcolm X, *The Autobiography of Malcolm X*, Grove Press, N.Y., 1964.

McWilliams, Carey, *Brothers Under the Skin*, Little, Brown & Co., Boston, 1951.

Mead, George H., *Mind, Self and Society*, University of Chicago Press, Chicago, 1948.

Mead, George H., *"Experimentalism as a Philosophy of History,"* in *The Philosophy of the Act*, University of Chicago Press, 1938.

Morison, Samuel Eliot, *The Oxford History of the American People*, Oxford University Press, N.Y., 1965.

Morison, Samuel Eliot and Henry Steel Commager, *The Growth of the American Republic*, Oxford University Press, 1962.

Morris, Desmond, *The Human Zoo*, McGraw-Hill, N.Y., 1969.

Morse, Arthur D., *While Six Million Died: A chronicle of American Apathy*, Random House, N.Y., 1968.

Myrdal, Gunnar, *An American Dilemma*, Harper & Bros., N.Y., 1944.

Myrdal, Gunnar, *Beyond the Welfare State*, Yale University Press, 1960.

*Partisan Review*, "Black Power: A Discussion," Spring, 1968.

*Psychiatric Aspects of School Desegregation*, Group for the Advancement of Psychiatry, Report No. 37, N.Y., 1957.

Quarles, Benjamin, *The Negro in the Making of America*, Collier Books, N.Y., 1968.

Rainwater, Lee and Yancey, William L., *The Moynihan Report and the Politics of Controversy*, MIT Press, Cambridge, Mass., 1967.

*Report of the National Advisory Commission on Civil Disorders*, Bantam, N.Y., 1968.

Riis, Jacob A., *How the Other Half Lives*, Hill and Wang, N.Y., 1957.

Rist, Ray C., "Student Social Class and Teacher Expectations: The Self-Fulfilling Prophecy in Ghetto Education," *Crisis in Urban Education*, op. cit.

Rogers, J.A., *Sex and Race*, 3 volumes, Helga M. Rogers, N.Y., 1944.

Salk, Erwin A., *A Layman's Guide to Negro History*, McGraw-Hill, 1967.

Scheinfeld, Amram, *The Human Heredity Handbook*, J.B. Lippincott, N.Y., 1956.

Schorr, Alvin L., "How the Poor Are Housed," *Poverty in America*, eds., Louis A. Ferman, Joyce L. Kornbluh, and Alan Haber, University of Michigan Press, Ann Arbor, 1965.

Schwartz, Barry N. and Disch, Robert, *White Racism*, Dell, N.Y., 1970.

Shaw, Clifford & McKay, Robert, *Juvenile Delinquency*, Revised Edition, University of Chicago Press, 1969.

Silberman, Charles E., *Crisis in Black and White*, Random House, N.Y., 1964.

Smith, Lillian, *Killers of the Dream*, W.W. Norton, N.Y., 1961.

Sullivan, Leon H., *Build Brother Build*, Macrae Smith Co., Philadelphia, 1969.

Terkel, Studs, *Division Street: America*, Pantheon Books, N.Y., 1967.

*Day They Marched, The*, ed., Doris E. Saunders, Johnson Publishing Co., Chicago, 1963.

*Federalist Papers, The*, Mentor, N.Y., 1961.

*Negro in Music and Art, The*, International Library of Negro Life and History Publishing Co., Inc., 1967.

*The Negro Heritage Library*, Educational Heritage, Inc., N.Y., 1965.

Thomas, Piri, *Down These Main Streets*, Signet, N.Y., 1968.

Thomas, W.I., *The Unadjusted Girl*, Little, Brown & Co., Boston, 1928.

Turner, Darwin T., and Bright, Jean M., eds. *Images of the Negro In America*, D.C. Heathand Co., Boston, 1965.

*Violent Crimes*, Report of the National Commission on the Causes and Prevention of Violence, George Braziller, N.Y., 1969.

Walton, Darwin, *What Color Are you?* An Ebony Jr. Book, Johnson Publishing Company, Inc., Chicago, 1973.

Washington, Booker T., *Up From Slavery*, Bantam, N.Y., 1967.

Weinberg, Meyer, *Desegregation Research*, 2nd Edition, Phi Delta Kappa, 1970.

Weinberg, Meyer, ed., *Learning Together:* A Book On Integrated Education, Chicago, 1964.

Wirth, Louis, *The Ghetto*, The University of Chicago Press, Chicago, 1966.

Wright, Richard, "Introduction," *Black Metropolis*, by St. Clair Drake and Horace Cayton, Harper Row, N.Y., 1945.

Wright, Richard, *Native Son*, Harpers, N.Y., 1940.

# INDEX

# INDEX

## A

Abortions, 95; U.S. Supreme Court, black attitudes toward, 119.

Adoptions, agencies, 95, 118.

*Aid to Families With Dependent Children*, 100-103.

Amendments, constitutional, intentions of 13th, 14th, 15th, 3; 45.

American, middle class, dream, 12, War of Independence, 62, opportunity structure, 73.

*American Civil Liberties Union*, 54.

Association, areas of, 10; and personal interchange, 10; interracial marriage, 115.

Attitudes, and values, 4; racial, 6, 7; changing, 7; anti-human, 56; changing racial, 78, 79, 82.

## B

Baldwin, James, quoted, 83, 129, 194.

Bertrand, Joseph, 80.

Black-belt, 15, see also Ghetto, 15.

Blacks, disabilities, proscribed group, achievement, potentials, black power, 5, 119; black pride, 5, 78, 116, 192; black experience, 129, 131; students, attitudes and Behavior of, 160; English language, 162-64; manners, 165-66 ff.; students, parents, school counselors, 174-76; friendships, black-white, 190-92; black teachers, 175-79, 193; harassment and conflict black-white, 184, 185, 190, 197, 206.

Blake, Eubie, quoted, 87.

Block-busting, 49, 54.

Boycotts, school, 5; consumer, 35, 103; Montgomery bus, 60, 61; business, schools, 71.

Bradley, Thomas, 82.

Broonzy, Big Bill, 117.

Brown, Claude, quoted, 183.

*Brown vs. Board of Education*, 3; see also U.S. Supreme Court decisions.

Busing, school, 126; resistance to, 128, 134; to maintain segregation, 129; teachers, black parents, 150-51. See also Court, U.S. Supreme and Courts Federal District.

# C

Capone, Al, 7.

Cayton, Horace, quoted, 45.

Chaney, James, 66.

*Chicago Property Owner's Journal*, 56.

*Chicago Daily News*, 56, 95.

Chicago, Illinois, 7; Hyde Park community of, 9; 10, 78, 126.

Children, adopted, interracial, identity, 117-18.

Cicero, Illinois, 7.

Clark, Jim, Alabama sheriff, 62.

Codes, legal, social, 4, 5.

Color, skin and hair texture, 4, 113-14, 106, 107; see also Race, Stereotypes.

Commanger, Henry Steele, quoted, 62.

Communication, interracial, 12; teacher and parents, 147., 152; teachers and, 177.

Community control, black demands for, 5, 152.

Constitution, preamble, 13th, 14th and 15th, Amendments, 4.

Consumers, ghetto, 33-35.

Court, United States Supreme, decisions, 3, 49, 61, 63, 94, 115, 119, 126, 129.

Eichmann, Adolph, 94.

Employment, blacks in, 9, 79; careers, 43; tokenism, 79. See also Stereotypes.

English language, black, white, standard, and stereotypic thinking, 162-64. See also Stereotypes.

Epstein, Paul A., quoted, 135.

Expectations, role, 3; revolution of rising, 77.

# F

Fair, Ronald, quoted, 107.

Families, ghetto, 35-43; black, harassment of, 47, 78.

Freedom Now, movement, 67, 71.

# G

Gangs, in the ghetto, names, as an institution, 18; English, German, Irish, Italian, Polish, 19, 20; transitional neighborhoods, 124.

Genocide, 94, 118, 119, 124, 174.

Germans, 33. See also Gangs, Housing.

Gettysburg, Lincoln's Address, 4; battle of, 73.

Ghetto, riots in, 5, 6, 73, 77, 78; community control, crime, public aid, 6; social problems, 6, 9; popular song, origin of term, Jews, involuntary confinement, black-belt; slum, anti-social behavior, 16; expansion, 47-57. See also Housing, Crime.

Goodman, Andrew, 66.

Gregory, Dick, 109.

# H

Havighurst, Robert J., quoted, 181.

Hitler, Adolph, 94.

Hopkins, Thomas, 38.

Housing, legislation, nation, state, 3; open occupancy, 7, 82; Cook County Department of Public Aid Study, 20; kitchenettes, 20-24; shortage of, 24; high-rise projects, 24-31; Germans & Irish, 33; seeking decent, 46, 54; public, 24-31; Fair Housing Act, 1968, 134-35; Home Investment Fund, Chicago Council on Religion and Race, 135; Housing and Urban Development, U.S. Department of, 24.

Hughes, Langston, quoted, 73, 155.

Hundt, Reed, quoted, 180.

# I

Ideas, unifying and school systems, 4, 121.

Identity, problems of, color, society and, 116 ff.

Immigrants, black, native and foreign-born white, 73.

Imperatives, legal, 3.

Inferiority, myth of, 3, 4; Slavic and Southern European, 31; black, 92, 93.

Integration, 12; meaning of, resistance to, 123 ff.; princi-

pals and, 199-204. See also Busing, Housing, Segregation Resegregation.

Ireland, 113.

Irish, 33; See also gangs and Housing.

# J

Jackson, Reverend Jesse, 47, 98.

Jackson, Maynard, 82.

James, William, 12, 96.

Javits, Jacob K., quoted, 123.

Jones, Reverend James G., Jr., quoted, 16, 20.

Johnson, Lyndon B., 134.

Julian, Percy, 80.

# K

Kennedy, John F., quoted, 66.

Kennedy-King College, 78.

Kerner, Otto, 6.

Kerner Report, *Report of the National Advisory Commission on Civil Disorders*, 6, 9, 77, 130.

King, Martin Luther Jr., 7; quoted, 12; assassination, 60, 134; Montgomery Improvement Association, 60, 61; Birmingham, Ala., 66; civil rights marches, 71.

Knights of Columbus, 80.

Ku Klux Klan, 60, 83.

# L

Law, segregation, due process, equal protection of, 3, 4; black experience and, 130-31; housing 71, 82; civil rights, 66; importance and effect of, 131, 134. See also Legislation and Courts.

Lawlessness, official, 62, 63.

Leadership, moral, 78.

Legislation, congressional, state, 3; civil rights acts, 1964, voting rights act, 1965, 66; open housing, 1968, 71, 82.

Lewis Oscar, quoted, 38.

Liberty Baptist Church, 7.

Living, conditions of, standards of, 4, 5. See also Housing, Stereotypes, Ghetto.

# M

Madison, James, 113.

Malcolm-X, quoted, 83; college, 78.

March on Washington, 12, 66.

Marches, open occupancy, hostility toward, 7; civil rights, 62.

Marriage, purpose of, interracial, 115.

Massialis, Byron G., quoted, 209.

Memphis, Tennessee, garbage workers, Martin Luther King, 60.

Migration, black, 6, 130; European, 73, 130.

Montgomery, Alabama, 60.

Montgomery Improvement Association, bus boycott, 60, 61.

Morals and morality, sexual behavior, pregnancies, abortions, prostitution, crimes, 94-96; marriage, 115, students, 170-74.

Morris, Desmond quoted, 10.

Morrison, Samuel Eliot, quoted, 63.

Motivation, blacks, black student, 110, 167.

Muhammed, Elijah, 84.

Myrdal, Gunnar, 12.

Myth, of inferiority, 5; psycholocigal effects of, 61.

# N

*National Association of Colored People*, 60.

*National Commission on the Causes and Prevention of Violence*, quoted, 19.

Negroes, 61, 62, 86, 127.

Neighborhoods, 45-47; and violence, 124, 125.

New York City, 19.

*New York Times*, 62, 118.

Nixon, Richard M., segregation, integration, law, 126.

Notions, primitive, tribal, 4.

# O

*Operation Breadbasket*, 98.

Opportunities, equal, denial of, 3, 4, 77; dreams of, 73; American structure & blacks, 73-82; increasing for blacks, 79; training for, 103.

*Opportunities Industrialization Center,*, 103.

# P

Panic peddling, 49, 53.

Parents, school, race, 4, 146, 147, 153, supra; and school counselors, 174-76.

Parks, Rosa, 60.

*People United to Save Humanity*, 34, 35, 98.

Philadelphia, Mississippi, 66.

Philadelphia, Pennsylvania, 103, 105.

*Plessy vs. Ferguson*, 66. See U.S. Supreme Court decisions.

Polarization, 10.

Power, black, 5, 119. See also Blacks.

Prejudice, black, 84; development of and ethnic, 88, 89-92; and the self, 92-93; and re-education, 209, 214-15.

Prophecy, self-fulfilling, 4.

Pride, black, 5, 78, 116, 192. See also Blacks.

# R

Race, "mongrelization," 55, racial stigma, 57; relations, black-white, 59, 78, 79 ff; seminars and staff develop-

ment, 204-05; race and color, genetic mixtures, 113-14; intermarriage, 115.

Racism, white, 6, 20; difference black, white, 84, 85, 86, 117-18; genocide, tokenism, 118-19; futility of, 210.

Reading levels, 10, 11.

Republican Party, national convention, 1960, 71.

Ready, R.K., quoted, 199.

Resegregation, 128, 169. See also Segregation, Resegregation, Integration.

Restrictive Covenant, 49.

Rights, equal; civil, 9; moral, legal, 47, 54; denial of, 61; civil rights marches, 66 ff.; constitutional, 3, 4, 62; civil rights acts 1964 & 1965, 66.

Riots, big city, 73, 77, 78; participants in, meaning of, causes of, aftermath of, 77, 78. See also Ghetto.

Riis, Jacob, quoted, 19, 33.

# S

Schwerner, Michael, 66.

Segregation, 6, 12; pattern of behavior, cause of ill-feelings, 59; effects of, 82, 83; color and, 113 ff.; 115, 123, 126, 131; *de facto*, and teachers, 180-81; 194. See also Courts, U.S. Supreme & Federal District.

Separatism, in schools, 205. See also, Demands.

Shakespeare, William, quoted, 59.

Slavery, stigma of, and ill-feelings, 61.

Smith, Lillian, quoted, 93.

Society, patterns of behavior, *mores*, social control, 3; integrated, segregated, 10.

*Southern Christian Leadership Conference*, 98.

Stereotypes, belief systems, prejudice, 88, 98; speech, 96-98) dress, 98-99; automobiles, 99; work and welfare, 99-105, 147; physical characteristics, 106-107; music, 108-09; sports, 109, 110.

Stokes, Carl, 82.

Sullivan, Leon H., quoted, 103; 105.

Sullivan, Leon H., quoted, 103; 105.

Superiority, white feelings of, self-examination, black rejection of, 86-93.

# T

Teachers, black students, need for approval, frustrations and effects of, 41-43, 156-158; stereotypes and inductive reasoning, 158-60, 164; students' expectations, 158, 160, 164; prejudice, discrimination, 173; teacher relations, 176-179; attitudes black parents, 146, 147, supra.

Thomas, W.I., 144.

Tokenism, racism and, 119; employment, 79.

Tulsa, Oklahoma, 131.

# U

Unemployment, 77, 103. See also Ghetto.

# V

Values, practical, behavior, 4; and manners, function of, 165-66 ff.

# W

Washington, Booker T., 115.

Watts, Los Angeles, California, 9.

Weinberg, Meyer, quoted, 127.

Welfare system, 15, 99-105; teachers, blacks and education, 147-149.

White Flight, 54, 56, 124.

Wille, Lois, 56, 95.

Workers, skilled, black, 4, 79, 99-100.

Wright, Richard, 118.

# ACKNOWLEDGEMENTS

The authors wish to acknowledge and express their deep appreciation for the encouragement offered them by the late Wayne D. Fisher, Professor, Foreign Language Education, University of Chicago; Leopold E. Klopfer, Professor of Education, University of Pittsburg; and Byron G. Massialis, Professor and Head, Department of Social Studies, Florida State University.

For continuing interest, encouragement and commitment the authors thank Robert J. Havighurst, Professor, Graduate School of Education, University of Chicago; Alison Davis, Professor, Psychology Department, University of Chicago; Benjamin Bloom, Professor, Graduate School of Education, University of Chicago; John Hope Franklin, Professor, History Department, University of Chicago; Timuel Black, Director, Community Affairs, City Colleges of Chicago; Joyce Clark, Coordinator, Higher Education Guidance Center Program, Chicago Public Schools; Ora Higgins, Assistant Personnel Director, Spiegels, Inc., Chicago; Charles Thomas, Superintendent of Schools, South Chicago School District; Pastora San Juan Cafferty, Assistant Professor, School of Social Services Administration, University of Chicago; and Eleanor Selk, Health Science Editor, Northwestern University.

We wish also to take this opportunity to express our appreciation to many employees (too numerous to mention individually) at the Cook County Department of Public Aid in Chicago, as well as to many public aid recipients, whose experiences and observations helped to form this book.

Special thanks go to James Hoge, Editor; Ralph Otwell, Managing Editor; Albert E. Von Entress, Vice-president, Circulation; Chan Forman, Magazine Editor; Tom Sheridan, Acting Features Editor, and Janet Polivka, Secretary — all of the *Chicago Sun-Times*, who made sure that the booklet, *If You're Going to Teach Black Students for the First Time* . . . got into the hands of their readers. Our thanks, too, to Janice Lewis, Librarian, and Tom Ray, Public Relations of the *Sun-Times* who aided us in obtaining many of the pictures used in *Breaking the Bonds of*

*Racism*. The help given by Bill and Edith Kelly of the Associated Press and Hank Schaeffer of United Press International with other pictures is also gratefully appreciated.

It is impossible to end the list of acknowledgements without mentioning at least some of our close friends and members of our family who have always been available to lend strength and wisdom whenever needed. They are Herbie Baler, Dr. W. John Weilgart, Yvonne Stevens, Phyllis Price, Mr. Kay of Camillia Fashions, Mike and Jean Binyon, Maxine Mitchell, Jean Favia, Richard Maskoff, Josephine Bland, Bruce McPherson (and all the former members of Checkerboard, Unlimited), Margaret Turner, Virginia Weimer Howarth, Patrick Weimer, Ray McCann, Norman Ross, Sarah Hodgkin, George and Patti Barr, Robert and Beverly Kennedy, Peggy Frazier, Buelah Jennings, Anna Gadsden, Mary Jane Odell, Loretta Joiner, Wayne Brasler, Pierre Bonvouloir, Donald O. Conway, Ella Cadet, Standrod T. Carmichael, Edwin C. "Bill" and Betsy Berry, Dr. Claude and Naomi Driskell, Mary Fisher, Fujii Klopfer, and the late Merlita Baham.

To our families for love, strength and guidance; to all our nieces and nephews, Paul's sister and brother-in-law, Charlesetta and Herbert Pruitt, and brother, Keith; Ouida's brothers, Clarence and Richard, her mother, Kathryn M. Hogan, with extra thanks to her sister Barbara Carter for dedicated late night typing of the manuscript.